TECHNOLOGY AND ITS DISCONTENTS:
THE DEADLY EMBRACE OF TECHNOLOGY AND
SOCIETY

L.V. Orman

TABLE OF CONTENTS

PROLOGUE

We are defined by the tools and technologies we use. They shape our identity. They feed and shelter us. But they also threaten our very existence. What separates us from all other animals is primarily the plethora of tools and technologies we created for our well-being and for our very survival. They are the source of our admirable success as a species; and they are the source of our most terrifying problems. Sometimes, they are the only solution to the very problems they created. That puts us in a race against ourselves, a race among technologies, a race between the good they do and the misery they cause, often the same technology doing both at different times and under different conditions. This has been the human condition from the beginning of our species, and it will likely be the human condition at the end.

Although we appear helpless, being dragged along a road carved by our own creations, there are some things we can do to minimize the risk to ourselves, without giving up all the advantages of a myriad of technologies we created. We may not be able to eliminate the basic paradox of human existence, but we may somewhat reduce the suffering. This book is about the beauty and the misery of our technological human society, offering some modest remedies for the misery, while praising the beauty.

PART 1
TECHNOLOGY AS THE DRIVER OF KNOWLEDGE, BELIEF, AND CULTURE

Not everything is technology, but often technology is everything.

A technology-driven society is in constant flux, and subject to accelerating change. In that environment, traditions, values, social institutions, and even complete cultures become obsolete at an increasing rate, and lose their value as inter-generational learning tools. This part describes the problem with numerous examples, and investigates possible solutions. A dynamic society with flexible and diverse social institutions is suggested as a possible solution. The solution itself requires an extensive technology infrastructure, and fundamental changes to the existing social institutions.

CHAPTER 1
TECHNOLOGY-DRIVEN SOCIETY

A technology-driven society is in constant flux, and subject to accelerating change. In that environment, traditions, values, social institutions, and even complete cultures become obsolete at an increasing rate, and lose their value as inter-generational learning tools. More importantly, since traditions, values, and social institutions are critical to human judgment and learning, when technology undermines our institutions, it also threatens our knowledge and beliefs. It challenges what we believe to be true, and what we believe to be relevant. That poses a fundamental challenge to the human society, since our knowledge and beliefs guide our behavior, and provide purpose in life. Losing our anchor to stable and universal truths leads to an unstable society, with no intergenerational continuity, where in fact the society is made anew by every generation [13].

There are three critical questions in such a dynamic technology-driven environment:
a. Why do we believe some things to be true and relevant, but not others? If it is technology driven, what technologies led to the current traditions, values, and the existing culture that makes some things relevant and true, but not others? This is a historical and descriptive question.
b. How do social institutions and cultures adapt as underlying technologies change? What is the process of adaptation? What are the institutional incentives, and do they coincide with the social interest? These are institutional and adaptation questions.
c. Are there better ways for social institutions and cultures to cope with technological change? Who benefits and who loses from these new approaches? Can we create incentives for institutions to behave differently, or even socially optimally? These are normative and design questions.
We will attempt to answer the first question in great detail in this part, and provide some tentative answers to the remaining two questions.

There are four major reasons why we believe some things to be true, but not others:

a. Universal truths and philosophical edicts,
b. Cultural imperatives and accidental beliefs,
c. Scientific truth and evidence based beliefs,
d. Self-serving beliefs.

We will see that none of these four reasons are reliable indicators of truth in a fast-changing, technology-driven society, which points to a fundamental problem with truth, belief, and knowledge in modern society. Modern social institutions are created to provide social stability, but that makes them very resistant to change. Social institutions typically have fixed and rigid rules of behavior that work efficiently in a stable environment, but become obsolete very quickly in a dynamic fast-changing environment. To further complicate the problem, institutions often have large constituencies and bureaucracies with their own interests, quite separate from the social interest that may have created the institution. As constituencies gain power, and bureaucracies are entrenched, their own interests tend to increasingly dominate the institutional decisions at the expense of the social objective. As institutions become obsolete, the values and knowledge they espouse and impart increasingly become irrelevant, misleading, or even false, leading to dysfunctional institutions, incorrect beliefs, and inconsistent and maladaptive behavior. We will make this case in the next four chapters. In the last chapter of this part, we will argue that there are solutions. It is possible to build flexible institutions that can change with the environment, and continue to serve their original purpose successfully, but those institutions would be drastically different from the current institutions. They would need to be designed explicitly for maximum flexibility, by explicitly recognizing the technologies that underlie their institutional assumptions, and by modifying those assumptions as the technological environment changes [2, 14].

CHAPTER 2
UNIVERSAL TRUTHS

Universal truths are what are accepted by all as fundamental reality of human existence. Philosophers have been investigating universal truths for millennia, and developed extensive theories and frameworks that define what is universally true and self-evident to all. The earliest examples of universal truth are god's word. But that is immediately recognizable as an oxymoron, since there is no universal religion and a universal god, and each religion proclaims different truths. A variation on god's word as universal truth is the suggestion that there are some basic moral tenets that are common to all religions. That also turns out to be incorrect. Let's take one of the most basic tenets such as the prohibition against killing. One does not have to go very far back in history to find many religions that approve or even require human sacrifice, specifically to appease gods. Mayan religions are good examples of this [37].

Moral philosophers have attempted to replace god's word with universal ethical principles that are observed by most human societies. However the existence of such moral principles is also suspect. Once again, prohibitions against killing may be a good example. Even such a basic and intuitive tenet is driven by specific technological and cultural conditions, and the tenet changes with technology and culture. First, even in our current culture, there are many exceptions to this rule, such as war, self-defense, and state sanctioned killing of criminals. More importantly, a rudimentary anthropological analysis shows that broad prohibitions against killing are fairly new in human history. Even in recent history, dueling was an acceptable practice in Europe, and it allowed killing within strict rules. Blood feuds were common in much of the world, where revenge killing was accepted and even expected. What is slightly more universal is the distinction between killing an in-group member, as opposed to killing an outsider, and prohibitions against killing within one's group. However, the definition and the boundaries of one's group identification is culturally and technologically defined, hence making even such a basic tenet quite fluid and variable depending on the available technologies. Human (and animal) existence can be characterized as a constant tug of war between cooperation within one's group, and competition outside of one's group, but the boundaries between the two constantly change. The in-group is defined by the need to maximize the benefit from cooperation and minimize the threat from competition. As technologies of cooperation make the individual more dependent on others, by allowing communication and coordination over larger groups and larger distances, and the technologies of competition make enemies more deadly and less predictable, the in-group expands [15].

Consider communication technologies like telephone and internet, and transportation technologies like highways and airplanes. They made economic and political alliances possible over larger distances, and with larger groups of people. That increasingly led to larger groups of identification. Early groups of identification in human history were based on blood kinship and physical proximity. But, the groups of identification expanded in direct proportion to the range of communication and transportation technologies, to villages, city states, nations, international alliances, and eventually the whole world. It is not an exaggeration to suggest that highways, railways, radio, telephone, and telegraph created national identities out of the previous tribal identities, and air travel, television, and internet created international and global identities out of the previous national identities. In societies where a national infrastructure was not built, due to geography, war, colonialism, or poverty, tribal identities remained dominant, as in Afghanistan, Libya, and Somalia. Similarly, the technologies of competition, such as the weapons of warfare, resource hoarding, and the ability to control water and food resources of others with dams, pollution, and industrial waste also increased the size of identification group. The end of colonialism for example can be directly tied to the increasing deadliness of weapons of war, and their wide spread availability, which made warfare more risky for all, and made political domination of other societies more costly. As a result, killing became increasingly unacceptable behavior for increasingly larger communities of identification, except for the most isolated and vulnerable; and was increasingly replaced with economic domination as in social classes and neocolonialism. The reduction of violence in human societies for the past millennium then is a direct result of the increasing deadliness of weaponry, not moral enlightenment [29].

Technologies of war often determine the community of identification. The invention of gun powder and placement of artillery on ships separated European empires from their African and Asian colonies. Nuclear weapons separate the developed nations from the developing. It is not an accident that the most prominent symbol of Christianity, the cross, is a technology of execution. It was designed by Roman Empire to torture and prolong suffering with a slow death from lung collapse and slow asphyxiation, and to display the slowly dying man to the masses. Other torture technologies were created by other cultures, reflecting their specific values, fears, and objectives. In the Balkans in the Middle Ages, they involved impaling people, by passing a long stick through their entire body, from anus to mouth, without killing them, and displaying them as they slowly died over days from internal bleeding. In China it was dripping water over a human body for weeks, as it created the sensation of drilling holes into the body and drove victims insane. All of these torture technologies fell out of use as social and economic integration of societies increased interaction and inter dependence among social groups, classes, and nations, and made it difficult to torture anyone without risking torture back. Torture is useful when torturer and the tortured belong to separate and isolated groups isolating the torturer from the threat of revenge. Modern transportation and communication technologies ended that isolation, and hence the practice, not any moral enlightenment [29].

Sudden technological collapse due to war, disease, or climate change can lead to societies that are almost unrecognizable to us as human societies. The Ik people of Northern Uganda are a good example of this. They have almost no group identity with almost no sharing. Each Ik will search for food and water alone and will never share it with anyone, not even with its siblings or parents. A sibling may die of starvation, while the other is very well nourished, but the healthy sibling will not assist the dying one. The same holds for married couples. They live together in the same location, but never share anything, or care for each other. Children are minimally cared for by their mothers until the age of three, and then set free to fend for themselves. They are expected to find their own food and shelter, and even protect themselves from adults, who will steal their food if the opportunity arises [38]. Even the most basic concepts of family, community, sharing, and cooperation are shaped by the technologies of specialization and interdependence, such as agriculture, hunting, and manufacturing.

More recent efforts to discover universal truths focused on universal human rights. If there are no universal ethical principles, maybe there can be universal agreement that humans have some inalienable rights in every decent society, with isolated exceptions. In fact any basic human right one can imagine appears to be an artifact of existing technologies and culture. That knowledge itself is acquired through the use of increasingly sophisticated technologies used to study archeological evidence, and its precision and reliability depends very much on the technologies available to investigate ancient cultures. As new technologies allow us to study increasingly ancient cultures, which existed within a drastically different technological environment than our own, we are able to see past our current biases and norms, and discover that all human values and beliefs are fundamentally culture and technology specific [11].

Consider prohibitions against slavery, incest, cannibalism, and rape which are all universal in the modern world. In fact, slavery as an institution existed longer than most of our current institutions. Enslavement of the losing side in warfare was routine for much of human history, following the invention of agricultural technologies. Similarly, rape was a natural part of warfare. Agricultural technologies made human labor a valuable property, and subsequent ownership of one's children as labor made fertile women valuable property. As valuable property, they became war bounty, after all the purpose of early warfare was to acquire valuable land and property. These were such established values that Alexander the Great used them as recruiting tools for his armies. His recruiters would promise all recruits that military service meant "all the food you can eat", and " all the sex you can have", since any victory brought in all the men of the enemy as slave labor, all their warehoused food as bounty, and all of their young women as sex objects. Incest turns out not to be a universal taboo either. In ancient Polynesian tribes where children were not owned by parents, but by the whole tribe, and sex was communal during "fertility dances", sex was not limited to unrelated partners. Actually, when parents do not own their children, they do not necessarily recognize them as their children, as in many other primate groups. In ancient Greece, there is evidence of sexual activity between parents and children, which makes its way into many mythologies. Cannibalism is similarly much more common than previously thought. Mayan and Aztec rituals involving "virgin sacrifices" appear to be much more than attempts to appease gods, but also to appease the priests. Evidence suggests that the priests that oversaw the sacrifice of young prepubescent girls may have regularly cooked them and eaten them, which suggests that they may have also been sex objects for the otherwise celibate and isolated priests, especially judging from the fact that beauty was one of the criteria for the selection of girls for sacrifice. All of these practices have disappeared with the social, economic, and political integration and interdependence of disparate social groups, where advantaged and disadvantaged, winners and losers, parents and children, priests and peasants could not be adequately separated, and protected from each other, due to more effective transportation, communication, agriculture, and warfare technologies [19, 37].

Moral philosophers continually attempt to discover frameworks, and formulate universal truths within each framework. A classic ethical dilemma involves a runaway train approaching a switch. On one side of the switch there are three people standing on the tracks; on the other side there is one person standing on the tracks. You control the switch, and the train is going to kill the three on the tracks if you take no action. Would you throw the switch to kill one person instead of three? Most people say yes to minimize the number killed. Then, the question is reformulated to require you to physically throw one person under the train, to stop the train and save the three on the tracks. Most people say no to that proposition. Philosophers muse at the inconsistency since the ethical problem appears to be the same. In fact, it isn't! First of all, this is a technology dependent question. Without a train technology, or a similar technology that enables such killing, the ethical dilemma would disappear. Second, since the subject does not know any of the people on the tracks, their value to the society, their interest in life, or any other facts about them, the subject is probably indifferent between the two options. It really doesn't matter to him. The questioner is prompting the response by suggesting that killing fewer people may be more desirable. Third, from a purely personal interest perspective the two options are not equivalent. Throwing somebody under the train involves considerable effort and risk to the subject. There is a real possibility that the person may fight back to save his life! Fourth, the obvious solution is in the technology itself. Most modern trains have break systems that would alleviate this ethical problem. The important point is that most ethical questions have technological origins, and technological solutions. They are neither universal nor intrinsic to the human condition.

CHAPTER 3
CULTURAL IMPERATIVES AND ACCIDENTAL BELIEFS

Every culture has its superstitions. Ours is no exception, with many arbitrary beliefs about the virtues of work, family, arts, education, sports, and charity, and about the evils of drugs, sex, money, and politics. In a different culture, you could easily find the opposite beliefs, as anthropologists often do, especially when they study ancient cultures. Humans have a need, and strong incentives to explain the world, even if the explanation is arbitrary, or even wrong. Explanations guide behavior; and as such they are useful even if they are wrong, if they lead to useful behavior. The mere predictability of behavior is useful, because it leads to social cohesion and trust, and potentially a more productive society. Beyond that, there are great advantages to be in a position to define what behavior is useful and desirable for everyone else, because that leads to power to control others' behavior, and make them to behave to serve someone else's interests.

A common superstition is the description of death as a journey to an unknown territory in each culture, given the existing technologies of that culture. Ancient Polynesians described death as a journey to a remote island in the Pacific. Pagans and monotheistic religions described death as a journey to the sky, because the islands of their world were already discovered and known. Modern new age religions sometimes describe death as a journey to another dimension, because the visible sky has largely been discovered and known. Every religious belief reflects the technologies available at the time. In monotheistic religions, god relies on human emissaries, called prophets, to communicate his message. That shows that the communication technologies available to god were very similar to what was available to humans at the time. In Judea-Christian-Moslem tradition, the story of Noah building a ship to rescue animals from a massive world-wide flood stands out as a prominent technological story. Yet, the story reflects the technologies available at the time. Building a ship, as opposed to an earlier technology of a raft, or a later technology of an aircraft, suggests that the technologies available to the prophet were similar to the technologies available to ordinary humans. Saving large animals, but not microscopic organisms, and the assumption that all large animals could survive on a ship, without an appropriate ecology of food, prey, insects, plants, and bacteria suggests that the prophet's knowledge of the biological world was similar to the ordinary humans at the time. Yet, the prophet made sure that there were two of each animal saved, reflecting the existing knowledge of reproduction at the time. No exceptions were made for self-fertilizing or cloning life forms like the lizard species leiolepis ngovantrii, earth worms or slime molds. No attempts were made to freeze sperms or eggs, or even save the genetic code of some species. God appears to be limited by the technological capabilities of the era [9].

Superstitions are not limited to religion. Any modern sports fan screaming at his television set, in the hope of influencing the outcome of the game through his ardent support of his team, is also subscribing to a superstitious belief system. Such a belief system is also the result of a technological environment that not only provides a communication tool for him to watch a remote game, but also creates the psychological and physical isolation typical of modern life, which creates the need to identify with a remote sports team. Technology creates the need by separating him from his social support group, such as an extended family, work group, or life-long friends; and technology satisfies the need by giving him an alternative, a sports team, that he can remotely follow, to alleviate his physical and psychological isolation. Humans have a fundamental need to belong to a group, like all other primates. How that need is satisfied is determined by available technologies [41].

Such cultural imperatives can become self-fulfilling prophesies. Romantic love is one of the most pervasive beliefs in modern world. So wide-spread is the belief, it is surprising that it is only a few hundred years old. Monogamy itself is a relatively new concept in human history, but romantic love as a basis of marriage is a Middle Ages European invention, specifically by French minstrels called Troubadours. Previously, marriages were arranged between families and tribes to forge social and economic alliances. The concept of choosing your own mate was novel at the time. Moreover, recognizing that mate as your "true love" after only a few brief encounters, and instinctively knowing that it is your "true love" from the feelings it generates, are common superstitions. Those feelings are expected to be quite different from any feeling you ever experienced with anybody else, and they are suggestive of super natural forces at work. Yet, we are advised that the feelings are real, and we will have them when we meet the "right person". Of course, anticipating such a supernatural event, and expecting such vaguely defined and unusual feelings, most everybody eventually feels it, fulfilling the expectations. In fact, romantic love is a modern invention created by the collapse of extended family, itself caused by the mobility required by an industrial society. You can't carry your extended family with you to that new job in a different town; but you could carry one mate with you, but then that relationship has to be all encompassing and deeply fulfilling to satisfy all of your emotional and physical needs. Once the need is created, the mass media, starting with the travelling minstrels of medieval Europe, and ending with movies and television programs of today, can easily create and spread such a mass superstition, and even one as dramatic and obsessive as romantic love [23, 32].

Self-fulfilling prophesies can become self-reinforcing when they are experienced repeatedly, and counter evidence is suppressed either accidentally or deliberately. Hammurabi, the famous Babylonian king, established a process of criminal trial. Suspected criminals were thrown into a crocodile infested river to establish guilt or innocence. The belief was that if he was innocent he would survive, but if he was guilty he would not. This belief served important goals of establishing an orderly process for criminal trials, and also deterring crime, irrespective of its truth and reliability. More importantly, the belief was self-reinforcing, because contrary evidence was always naturally suppressed. The guilty who survived had no incentive to talk; and the innocent who died were not alive to talk. So nobody could reasonably challenge the system. Most interestingly, the system was completely dependent on the existing fishing and hunting technologies, as the probability of survival was directly proportional to the number of crocodiles in the river, and the availability of other food sources to maintain that crocodile population. It is reasonable to assume that as the crocodiles were hunted down due to better hunting technologies, and their food source of fish and turtles were depleted due to better fishing technologies, the survival rates for suspects must have improved dramatically, undercutting the crime deterrent value, and forcing an end to the practice. Major changes in technology are often the only way to end self-reinforcing beliefs [4].

Similar self-reinforcing beliefs exist in modern societies. Modern judicial process is very similar to Hammurabi's in its superstitious and self-reinforcing quality. Modern criminal trials are based on the assumption that an adversarial process, where the two opposing parties make the best case for their side, will lead to the emergence of truth from that debate. It is not clear how the truth can emerge from such an adversarial proceeding, when nobody has the incentive to make the case for the actual truth. Truth is nobody's friend in an adversarial proceeding, since everybody has an incentive to bend the truth in their direction, to the best advantage of their side. And everybody in the legal profession agrees that winning is critically dependent on the oratory and legal skills of the lawyers, notwithstanding the fact that lawyering skill has nothing to do with the truth! The belief is self-reinforcing, because winners have no incentive to challenge the system; and the losers are discredited as guilty, and have no credibility to challenge the system; and the legal profession is dependent on the system for its livelihood, and has no incentive to challenge the basic assumptions of the system. Such elaborate systems of truth seeking are a result of our inability to develop technologies that can directly seek truth. Technologies that identify and detect the human physiology of truth telling are in development and utilize a variety of techniques from detecting skin temperature and pupil dilation to reading brain waves. An effective technology to detect the physiology of truth telling is likely to end all adversarial systems of truth seeking [33].

Self-reinforcing beliefs are very common. For much of American history, homosexual sex acts were considered unnatural, dirty, and immoral. In some states like North Carolina in 1800's, you could potentially be executed for engaging in homosexual sex acts. The original reason for the prohibition may have been the importance of reproduction in a labor intensive economy and defense, and also the higher risk of infection with some homosexual acts. But those beliefs were self-reinforcing, since prohibition itself pushed homosexuals underground, and forced them to take higher risks through anonymous sexual liaisons, and more reluctance to seek medical care, reinforcing the belief that homosexual acts were unnatural, dirty, and immoral. Most importantly, the original arguments for prohibition were technology dependent. As industrial revolution diminished the need for labor both in economic activity and in warfare, a large population actually became a liability, and reproduction lost its prominent role in social welfare. Moreover, the technologies of indoor plumbing, hot showers, condoms, and antibiotics greatly reduced the risk of infection from sexual activity. Hence the reasons for prohibition disappeared with new technologies. That is probably the main factor in achieving gay rights, rather than any sudden political enlightenment. Women's rights movements were similarly impacted by birth control technologies, and the need for labor in factories during the Second World War, which reportedly pushed women out of the home and into professional careers. Those technological changes were necessary to overcome the self-reinforcing beliefs about women's inability to perform at factories and professional jobs, and their inability to dedicate themselves to professional careers. The beliefs were self-reinforcing because women derived their social value primarily from motherhood and homemaking, and only those who failed at those more valuable occupations went into factory jobs or professional careers. And even those women aspired to leave their jobs and go back to homemaking, leading to high rates of failure, which reinforced the original belief. Major technological changes were necessary to break the self-reinforcing cycle [8].

Self-reinforcing beliefs can easily turn into vicious cycles when the reinforcement strengthens the belief, not just maintain it. Blood feuds that dominated tribal societies are classic examples of vicious cycles. When everybody believes that any wrong against you has to be responded in kind, and with additional ferocity, than any wrong has the potential to explode exponentially into a feud. An eye for an eye, or worse, two eyes for an eye, is destined to lead to a vicious cycle, leaving everybody blind. The original reason for such a strategy was probably maximum deterrence, and it may have worked when the weapons available were crude with limited damage to specific individuals. With increasing deadliness of weaponry, such feuds could easily wipe out complete communities, and that is probably why the practice has largely been abandoned. Similar arguments apply to nations using fierce retaliation against any incursion against their national interest. That strategy may have been effective in an earlier era when wars were limited geographically and politically. In a nuclear era that strategy is largely abandoned, and replaced with controlled de-escalation, and no nuclear weapon has ever been used against a rival with nuclear weapons. Once again, technology determines the viability of the strategy [15].

Similarly, the modern belief that teenagers are rebellious and immature leads parents to monitor them closely, and restrict their freedom. That leads teenagers to even more immature and rebellious behavior, since it is difficult to tolerate being treated like a child well into your teens. The vicious cycle continues with even more strict regulation and monitoring of teen age lives, often with the help of law enforcement such as curfews, drinking age laws, and sexual age of consent laws, which reinforce the cycle. Most interestingly, this vicious cycle was set off originally by increasing educational demands, and decreasing labor requirements of an industrial society, which extended schooling for most everybody into their 20's, not because any changes in the maturity or reliability of teenagers. The vicious cycle will probably be broken only when new communications and social networking technologies will empower teenagers to organize and challenge the strict regulation and monitoring of their lives [8, 10].

National economies fall into such vicious cycles also. There is a wide spread belief in the Western World that markets are efficient and lead to prosperity and growth, despite some mixed evidence from Africa and Latin America, and despite recurring financial crises in the developed economies. More interesting to observe is the huge rewards conferred by markets to successful businesses, and the immense sizes those businesses can achieve. One can easily witness this in giant oil companies like Exxon-Mobil, giant banks like Citibank, and giant internet companies like Google and Amazon. Ironically, size confers market power, and allows them to grow further, by using financial power to eliminate or absorb competitors, and by using political power to influence government policy to gain advantages over competitors. No business likes to be in a head-to-head competition with a large number of competitors in a perfect competition that economists describe and idealize. A completely unregulated economy then, can easily get into such a vicious cycle, and the marketplace ends up being dominated by a few very large firms, as happened in early 20th century America with oil, steel, and railroad monopolies. Such vicious cycles are very difficult to break, without government intervention, or without fundamental changes in the dominant technologies. Major changes in technology may allow the smaller firms to break the monopolies of dominant firms, but only if the dominant firms fail to recognize the technological change and fail to take advantage of it. Even then, the change is chaotic, and the new successful firms quickly grow, and using the same strategies, can become the new monopolists [18].

The story of Google breaking the dominance of Microsoft is such a story when Microsoft failed to recognize the importance of the internet in 1990's, and left an opening for a new search engine to dominate that market. The rise of Toyota as a major automobile company is another example of how General Motors failed to recognize the importance of new technologies to build cheap and fuel efficient cars in 1960's, and left that originally unprofitable market to a new company called Toyota. As the technology of building cheap and fuel efficient cars improved, that market increasingly moved into the established mainstream automobile market, and destroyed GM's dominance. These are typically called disruptive technologies, because they are originally not competitive and easily ignored by the dominant firm. However such disruptive technologies are not common; and vicious cycles dominate markets, and maintain the power of dominant firms. More interestingly, new web-based technologies may help dominant firms to consolidate their power by preempting disruptive technologies. They can do this by operating in multiple markets simultaneously without cannibalizing their existing markets, by using customization and price discrimination. Web based technologies are very useful for learning about many diverse customer segments, for customizing products for each, and for isolating customer segments from each other with customized marketing messages and different pricing strategies, while allowing different business units within the company to cooperate and take advantage of synergies among otherwise distinct business endeavors. To see a company like Google operate in so many markets from search to advertising, and from cloud services to phone operating systems, to block any possible disruptive technology, is very informative [7].

Similar arguments apply in explaining why prestigious universities remain prestigious, and second rate colleges cannot improve their standing no matter how hard they try. Prestigious universities attract the best professors, best students, and the most grants; and that only reinforces their position, and allows them to improve their reputation even more, and dominate their niches. Prestige is a collective belief that reinforces itself. With online education, this trend is likely to intensify, with a few prestigious universities dominating the whole higher education business, by providing distant education and credentials to all, since distance and physical facilities will not be a limiting factor anymore. On the other hand, new web based technologies provide an opportunity for new educational models and institutions to gain a foothold, by first providing an inferior product that leaders may ignore, and later as the technology improves, make inroads into mainstream education and challenge the leaders. This is the classic disruptive technology argument described above, and requires complacence on the part of the leaders to succeed. Similar arguments apply to celebrity and fame [7].

CHAPTER 4
SCIENTIFIC AND EVIDENCE-SUPPORTED BELIEFS

Scientific belief is not as universally reliable as often assumed, but instead it is often technology and culture specific. This is especially true with social sciences, and sometimes leads to dangerous mistakes when beliefs are used to guide behavior and policy. There are multiple reasons for such failures:

a. Selection problem suggests that what scientists select to study and what they choose to report greatly biases their findings towards their existing beliefs and their culture. b. Sufficiency problem suggests that the criteria used to decide how much evidence is sufficient to believe and trust the findings may not be sufficiently stringent, and also limited by the technologies of data collection, analysis, and experimentation. c. Relevance problem relates to who the findings apply to. All scientific findings hold under certain assumptions, and those assumptions are rarely universal, but culture and value specific. d. Evidence and data-based reasoning often finds relationships, but does not answer the "why" question, or establish causality. Without knowing why something happens, or what causes it, the knowledge gained from mere observations is often suspect, subject to interpretation, and specific to prevailing conditions. We will consider each in detail.

a. Scientists study issues that are considered relevant and important within the culture they exist. For example, there is a great deal of research effort and funds dedicated to studying the efficiency of markets by economists, and the effectiveness of democracies by political scientists. Yet, there is little interest in studying the efficiency of dictatorships, and the effectiveness of tribal societies. It is not because they are inherently inefficient and ineffective, but it is in nobody's interest to challenge our most basic cultural biases, or to invent new systems that might undermine all of our existing institutions. When scientists challenge existing dogmas, it is often done in the context of one powerful institution challenging another, not as a lone scientist challenging the dogma of a whole institution. Researchers are also limited in their vision by their technological and cultural environment. There is considerable research in economics and finance for example, that shows that markets are remarkably efficient. Yet, efficiency, defined as efficient allocation of resources, curiously excludes the institutional cost of the markets themselves. It appears that researchers have collectively decided that efficient allocation of resources is important irrespective of the cost of achieving that goal. This would be equivalent to judging a car by its fuel efficiency and horse power, irrespective of its price. And the cost of creating efficient markets is high, especially when one considers the cost of maintaining a banking and investment system. Of course, these biases were created at a time when the economy was dominated by manufacturing; and banking and investment were a negligible part of the overall economy. Today, making the markets efficient might very well be costing more than the value of that efficiency, but it is not known for sure, since it is not selected as a subject of intense scrutiny by the scientists [14].

Hard sciences are not immune from this problem. Physics has been very successful as an academic discipline in discovering "universal" rules of nature. Yet, new discoveries show that declaring the laws of physics "universal" may have been premature. New evidence suggests that laws of physics may apply only in human scales that scientists chose to study. At very small and also very large scales, the laws may be drastically different. The first signs of this possibility appeared as quantum mechanics challenges the established laws of physics in gravity, magnetism, and electricity. More recent findings suggest that even the speed of light may be different at very small scales. Similarly at very large scales, it is not even clear if the universe is really three-dimensional and finite as it is generally assumed at human scales [36].

There are similar problems in biology. Darwin's theory of evolution is hailed as the biggest revolution in biology. Yet, evolution may often be working in fundamentally different ways than Darwin suggested. There is some evidence that genetic mutations may not be completely random, but targeted and purposeful. That gives organisms some control over evolution, rather than leaving the whole process to the whims of natural selection. Most recent findings suggest that even the life time experiences of an individual organism may be passed on to its progeny through a gene activation mechanism. In effect, organisms may have some control over what genetic variations to activate, and what genetic variations to pass on the next generation, above and beyond just surviving and passing on random mutations. But the technologies necessary to discover those capabilities of organisms, such as gene mapping, were not available to Darwin, who was limited only to direct human observations. Technologies limit what scientists can observe and experiment with, which limits what they can study, and what they choose to study [5, 34].

Technologies even determine what humans are capable of comprehending and studying. It is widely acknowledged that the invention of fire and the related technologies of food preparation were critical to the success of human species. But it is not widely known how critical those technologies were to increasing the intellectual capabilities of humans, so that they could comprehend and communicate much more complex concepts, relative to their ape-like ancestors. Before fire, all food was consumed raw, as every other species still does, as this technology is unique to humans. Raw foods are much more difficult to digest, and human ancestors had a much more exaggerated digestive system to accomplish that, and spent a great deal of energy merely digesting food. Cooking technologies, and the resulting easy-to-digest cooked foods eventually reduced the size of the human digestive system, and dramatically reduced the energy required to digest food. It may take for example almost 40% less energy to digest cooked meat and vegetables, as opposed to eating them raw. That excess energy went to maintaining a much larger brain, since the larger brain was a competitive advantage, and the excess energy made it possible. In short, the remarkable brain power of humans is largely the result of a rather simple and early technology in human development: fire and cooking.

Before we get overconfident about our intellectual capabilities, it is important to remember that, even with our formidable intellectual capabilities, we understand very little about our physical environment. A good example is the philosophical concept of free will, our ability to make decisions and act on them freely and on our own. Even such a basic concept is very poorly understood. The concept is critical to our social existence since without it there would be no concept of social responsibility and punishment. What is the point of telling people what they can and cannot do, and rewarding and punishing them, if they have no control over what they do? But the very existence of free will violates the laws of physics, since if individuals have free will and can act freely on their own, then it suggests that the previous state of the universe cannot dictate the next state even probabilistically or even randomly, because if it did, the individual would have no choice but follow the dictates of the physical laws.

Let's explore this further since it is a little disconcerting. Imagine you are building a robot, and you would like it to have free will. How would you build it? A robot or a human can behave in three different ways, and none of them gives it free will:

I. Automatic behavior. You program it and the robot does it. Our heart works like this. It is programmed to beat in a certain way, and you have no conscious control over it. Similarly, our digestive system works like this, since you have no control over what happens to your food after you eat it!

II. Choice behavior. The robot observes its environment and takes a different action depending on the conditions. This is similar to our eating behavior, depending on how much hunger we feel, what food is available to us, and what tasted good in the past. Learning is also a type of choice behavior, because learning modifies your future behavior, but how you learn is itself programmed into you. You can even modify the learning algorithm, but how you modify would have to be programmed into you, ad infinatum.

III. Random behavior. The robot makes random choices, similar to our taking a walk and following a random path. But the random choice algorithm would have to be programmed into the robot.

None of these three options gives the robot free will. If a robot or a human has some capability to act independent of external input, we don't know how that is possible, and we have no way finding out with our current technologies. So, our best bet is that we are machines acting out our preprogrammed behaviors; but that goes against our intuition about ourselves, since we all think that we control our own behavior beyond following some built-in algorithm. It also challenges all of our human institutions, and the very basic social concepts of responsibility, justice, punishment, and reward.

Similarly, consider the biological sensations of pain and pleasure. What are they? Scientists tell us we experience them in our brain. What we experience in our brains is the knowledge that a certain sensation occurred in our nervous system. What we experience in our nerves is an electrical impulse, and that is recognized and classified as a certain type of nerve activity in the brain. None of this tells us where that sensation of pleasure or pain comes from. How does the mere knowledge that you experienced pain translate into that severe sensation of discomfort, agony and doom? It is not known! In other words, we could potentially build a robot that would sense changes to its body through sensors, such as the burning of its fingers. We could potentially equip the robot with processing power that analyzes the sensor output and classifies it as pain. But we have no way of building a robot that actually have a sensation of pain, because we don't know what that is; we wouldn't know how to build it; and we wouldn't know where to put it! Our available technologies severely limit what is known and what is knowable!

b. Even when the right issues are studied, scientific findings are not always reliable. Consider the 2009 study conducted by Cornell psychologist Daryl Bem. In a series experiments, he showed with significant statistical confidence that people can see the future and predict random future events. This finding violates physical laws of cause and effect, so one has to choose between the laws of physics as we know them, and the statistical confidence tests employed by psychologists. The more reasonable choice here is that the statistical confidence tests employed by psychologists are probably not stringent enough, especially because many researchers may conduct the same tests, and only those who discover unexpected results report them [1].

Statistical analysis is severely limited by the technologies of data collection and analysis, and fails frequently, when data collected is not representative of the relevant population, or the analysis is not theoretically sound, or the results are not significant statistically or practically. The most dramatic examples of statistical failure are in risk measurement. In finance, insurance, and disaster planning, researchers try to assess the probability of failure in a systematic fashion, by looking at past events, and use those to predict future events. That invariably underestimates the probability of extremely rare events, especially if they never happened before. Available technologies limit how far back you can look for data, and that limits what rare events you can predict. Disaster preparation specialists talk about 100-year or 200-year disasters, but it is impossible with current observation technologies to intelligently talk about a 10 thousand-year disaster, or to predict a financial crisis that has never happened before such as all developed economies defaulting on their national debt all at once, or a highly infectious new variant of the flu virus taking advantage of the global mobility of the world population and infecting 100% of the world population. It is impossible to intelligently predict such rare events with available technologies. On the other hand, current technologies allow increasingly accurate predictions of hurricanes and volcano eruptions. Technologies determine what we know about the future, and how accurate and reliable that information is [16, 39].

c. Even when the right problems are studied, and reliable results are obtained, it is often not clear how relevant those results are and to whom. For example, there is wide-spread agreement that air travel is safer than automobile travel. The statistics show that more people die in automobile accidents than in airplane accidents. But that fact alone may not be very meaningful. First of all there are more miles travelled by car than by plane, so the accident rates have to be normalized to per mile travelled. But that may not be meaningful either, since a typical car trip is much shorter than a plane trip, so normalizing the accident rates per trip may be more appropriate. But that will only help if planes and automobiles are actually available as alternatives for a given trip. They are not always. A trip to the grocery store cannot be taken by plane; or the trip to Europe cannot be taken by car; so the relative safety is not a meaningful concept for those trips. But how do we compare different modes of transportation in terms of safety then? Relative safety can only be relevant when we are comparing two modes of transportation for a particular trip to decide which mode to take. The fact that there are lots of accidents in the grocery store parking lot is not relevant to the decision involving a European trip. One would need to make the comparison for comparable trips where the alternatives are available. Even if a careful analysis could resolve all of these issues, the average accident rates may not be relevant to a particular traveler. The average accident rates apply to an average driver and an average pilot, but very few drivers are actually average. Some are better drivers; some are worse. Their results would be very different from the average driver. Although fliers do not have a choice of their pilot, so relying on the average accident rates may be reasonable for them; drivers control their own destiny, and the quality of drivers may be much more variable than the quality of commercial pilots, so the average rates may not be very reliable for them. Finally, to make the comparison almost impossible, safety technologies are not static. Every new model of a car, and every new generation of planes have new safety technologies; not to mention the changes to highway safety, road design, police presence, airport design, air traffic control technologies, radar equipment on the planes, automatic collision avoidance technologies, and a plethora of other technologies change the relevant factors. In a highly technological and fast changing society, past statistics are almost never relevant to future events [16, 39].

The same arguments also apply in finance. A particular individual's stock investment returns are not likely to match the stock indexes, because very few individuals are actually "average" investors. An individual investor is actually always at a disadvantage as compared to institutional investors, because the technologies and information available to each are quite different. Moreover, financial engineering technologies are constantly changing, so the past may not be a good predictor of the future. Financial crises almost always involve new financial instruments that have not been thoroughly tested, well understood, and carefully regulated. The great depression of 1920's followed the introduction of new technologies such as electrification, motorized transportation, and mass production, all of which increased productivity and decreased the demand for labor. Increasing productivity by replacing labor with capital boosted the demand for capital, and easy business and farm credit policies fueled the uncontrolled growth of the economy in 1920's, leading to the great crash. All of those, combined with a failure to understand the complex technology of money, and its subsequent lax regulation exacerbated the crisis and led to bank runs and bank failures, lack of investment, and persistent unemployment. Similarly, the savings and loan crisis of 1990's followed the introduction of new financial instruments allowing the conversion of real estate loans into government-backed bonds, and the weakening of government regulations. The great recession of 2008 followed the introduction of complex derivatives such as subprime mortgage-based securities and credit default swaps, and elimination of Glass-Steagall banking regulations. The new technologies of high-speed trading and 24-hour distant trading are likely to lead to new types of crises that are difficult to foresee. It is reasonable to conclude that we rarely get the same crisis twice, yet it is very difficult to anticipate completely novel crises. Crises are always technology and culture specific, and the assumptions made during the last crisis may not apply during the next one [17, 39].

More importantly, what we measure may not be relevant at all to what we intended to measure. Economic growth is often used as an indicator of economic well-being. Yet, it often is not; let alone being an overall indicator of well-being including psychological and medical. Drinking water used to be free, to be taken from any creek or lake as desired. Then we polluted our creeks and lakes; so now we have to purchase filtered and bottled water, and the payments we make count as economic growth since they add to the GDP. Paying for what used to be free is measured as economic growth, yet it is not clear why that would add to anybody's economic well-being.

d. "Correlation does not imply causality" is the rallying cry in social sciences. Yet, correlation is rarely useful. Only causality is meaningful in decision and policy making. For example, the fact that 50% of marriages end in divorce is not very helpful, unless we know why. The critical "why" question cannot ordinarily be answered simply by data analysis. Social scientists created ingenious ways to elicit causality from data analysis, but failures are common. One technique is to discover "natural experiments" where data is available in two different contexts, where all variables are the same except for one. Another technique is to use the knowledge of physical world to exclude all causal explanations except one. But it is never clear if all other variables and all other explanations have been excluded, to make a clear case for one. For example there is a correlation between exercise and longer life; there is a correlation between watching TV and autism; there is a correlation between age of marriage and the likelihood of divorce. However it is never clear if there is a causal relationship in any of these cases. Even if there is a causal relationship, it is not clear if first causes the second, the second causes the first, or a third factor causes both of them. Some scholars suggest that everything we know in social sciences is suspect, and a great deal of knowledge in physical and biological sciences that is based on data analysis is also unreliable [28].

Even when controlled experiments are conducted, and all variables are deliberately kept constant, varying only the relevant variables and observing outcomes, there are many problems. First of all, it is very difficult to conduct experiments with human subjects. It is sometimes illegal or considered immoral to conduct experiments with humans; and when it is done, it is rarely clear if a representative sample has been taken out of the relevant population, or if the participants are honestly cooperating with the experiment. For example, medical experiments are conducted with human subjects to test the efficacy of various drugs. Yet, the people chosen are often desperately sick to bypass prohibitions against experimenting with humans, or they are volunteers, both of which bias the results. More importantly, experiments with human subjects often involve asking them to record their experiences, like their medical symptoms, or products they use, or foods they eat; or they require them to take certain actions regularly, like taking a pill or exercising. Compliance with such extensive requirements is always suspect without extensive monitoring. Even if the participants are honest with the experimenters, human subjects often have faulty recollections, or incorrect self-images. For example, if you ask people about their level of pain and discomfort after surgery, you get very unreliable responses. The studies show that arthroscopic knee surgery for arthritis of the knee is very effective in reducing pain as reported by the patient. However, when a double-blind controlled study was conducted with two groups of patients, where one group received the surgical intervention, but the other group received a sham surgery involving just a skin incision, both groups reported the same level of reduction in pain. Other studies suggested that a third of all such surgical improvements maybe due to a placebo effect where the patient feels better just because of the expectation of feeling better after a surgical intervention, not because of any particular physical improvement [40].

Relying on this finding, a Persian doctor named Fereydoon Batmanghelidj achieved world-wide fame in 1980's when he started curing a variety of diseases by simply prescribing water. His "water treatment" received wide-spread acclaim, and he developed complex techniques involving various dosages and regimens of water for a variety of illnesses. There is evidence that the more complex the regimen, and the more technology intensive the intervention, the stronger the placebo effect, indicating the awe inspiring effect of technology and complexity on patients [40].

Similarly, if you ask people what television shows they watch, their responses are very different from the actual shows they watch. The answers reflect what they think they should be watching, like news and documentaries, as opposed to what they may actually be watching like reality shows and quiz shows. The availability of monitoring technologies such as sensors and cameras often determine the level of compliance and the reliability of the results. The quality of data collected often is also very sensitive to the availability of data collection technologies such as sensors and recording devices [16].

Hard sciences claim to be more reliable when they study underlying processes, rather than just observe outcomes and make statistical inferences. For example, whether television watching causes autism or not can only reliably be ascertained by studying and understanding the underlying brain processes that lead to autism. Whether exercise leads to longer life can only be reliably established by studying and understanding physiology of exercise and the process of aging. Whether the age of marriage may be causing divorce can only be decided by studying and understanding the dynamic processes of marriages, and the processes that lead to divorce. These types of studies are sometimes undertaken in anthropology to compare and contrast social processes. Once again, technologies available to dissect and observe processes are critical to success.

But, studying processes is difficult and time consuming. Studying outcomes is a cheaper and quicker alternative, and provides a great temptation for the researchers who are under pressure to publish. Late Harvard economist John Kenneth Galbraith famously lamented the transformation of the field of Economics from a field studying the economic processes, as they do in Anthropology, to a field observing the outcomes and doing empirical data analysis to discover relationships. He lamented that the field was impoverished by this development, as scholars in the field had become more tool experts, and less process and economic insight experts. Tools of course, are technology driven, and change constantly, and the body of knowledge becomes hostage to the vagaries of the available technologies of data collection, analysis, and experimentation [14].

Even when the processes are studied and understood, they often merely explain one unknown process in terms another. Technologies of observation often determine and limit the extent of our knowledge of processes. Consider the origins of universe. Physicists' answer to this question involves the "big bang" theory, and a process of expansion of the universe henceforth. But as careful as they are in studying the process, their explanation hardly answers the question. Since the big bang requires the existence of a black hole which is some concentrated mass, the origin of that mass remains unexplained. It merely explains one unknown, the universe, in terms of another unknown, the black hole. It explains the process hence, but not the process before. The technologies of observation often determine how far we can go in observing and explaining a process, and at what point we are blocked from observing further [36].

Similarly, biologists' explanation of the origins of life on earth suffers from the same shortcomings. Biologists point to the theory of evolution to explain origins life. But once again, as careful as they are in studying and explaining the process of evolution, their explanation hardly answers the question. Evolution requires a genetic code to be replicated, mutated, and selected for. It explains the process starting with primitive one-celled organisms and ending with the diversity of life we have now. But it does not explain the transition from inorganic material with no genetic code, to the primitive organisms with a genetic code that can be replicated, and have an incentive to be replicated. The creation of the genetic code is where our knowledge stops, and scientists are forced to speculate. Once again the technologies limit how far we can go in understanding the process, and the point at which we are blocked from observing further [5].

CHAPTER 5
SELF-SERVING BELIEFS

Beliefs guide actions, so there is an incentive to control what people believe, which leads to controlling their behavior, to ensure that it serves community interests, or the interests of those doing the controlling. Some people cynically control others' beliefs and behavior to serve their own interests. But most people simply convince themselves that what is good for them must also be good for everybody else, because that is psychologically more comfortable than cynically manipulating others, and accepting yourself as a liar and a hypocrite. It is not an accident then that the wealthy tend to be more libertarian, believing in less economic regulation by the government; and the poor tend to be more egalitarian, believing in social safety programs [30].

Consider the abortion debate that has dominated the American social agenda for a generation. The debate centers on when life begins, at conception, at birth, or at some other point like the end of first trimester. Different groups believe that life starts at different points in human development, and all groups point to science to bolster their arguments. But a quick analysis of the politics of the issue suggests that the debate may not be about the science of when life begins. There seems to be an unusual correlation between people's belief of when life starts and their political interests, which suggests that the real debate may be a political one, not a scientific one. It is not a coincidence then that professional women mostly believe that life starts at birth; and housewives and stay-at-home mothers mostly believe that life starts at conception. People's beliefs are often self-serving, and one can identify the political struggle by observing who believes what, and then working backwards from their beliefs to their political interests. Women's professionalization created an enormous economic and social advantage for highly-educated professional women, and made it increasingly difficult for less-educated housewives to compete. Professional men tend to prefer marrying professional women who contribute to the family income; and hence it is increasingly difficult to make a living as a stay-at-home mother and a housewife. Only a generation ago, a pretty face and a pleasant personality guaranteed women a life-long job as a housewife and a mother. Not anymore. In a competitive world, an increase in choices is not always good for everyone. Your increasing choices often limit other people's choices, by changing the competitive environment, and forcing people into competition that were not previously competing, or new types of competition that did not exist before. Abortion helps professional women by freeing them from unwanted pregnancies, and further advances their formidable advantages over housewives. The ensuing political struggle continues to this day, but it was triggered by a number of critical technologies. Technologies that allowed professionalization of women are many. They range from the automation of factory work which eliminated physical ability arguments, to automation of housework that diminished the value and prestige of housework and child rearing. Abortion and birth control technologies also helped by freeing women from unplanned pregnancies. Technologies created this debate. New technologies will probably end this debate, not political victories. The debate will end when birth control technologies are perfected to make abortion unnecessary; and when housework is almost completely automated or outsourced to professionals such as house cleaners, restaurants, and grocery stores; and child rearing is increasingly professionalized with extensive day care, night care, and long-term care. At that point, full time house work as a job will be increasingly untenable, and professionalization of women will have completed its technologically destined trajectory [8, 35].

Similar unending debates take place in economics. Markets versus governments is the age-old debate between those who believe that markets are efficient and lead to prosperity, and those who believe that markets are inefficient and lead to crises, but governments are effective and lead to stable growth. For every economist who points to the triumph of market economies in the US and Japan, there are economists who point to the successes of government planning in China and South Korea. But a quick analysis suggests that the debate is not an economic debate, but a political one. It is not a coincidence that wealthy and successful overwhelmingly believe that markets are efficient and dynamic, and the governments should stay out of economic planning and regulation; yet the poor and working classes overwhelmingly believe that governments are effective and fair, and markets should be heavily regulated to prevent the powerful from exploiting the powerless. People tend to believe what serves their economic and political interests. Truth is probably somewhere in the middle, but truth is often nobody's friend, because truth serves nobody's political interests completely and unconditionally [6].

Markets probably not as efficient as advocates claim. Large swings in stock prices or commodity prices suggest that markets are not very efficient, at least in the short run. If markets were perfectly efficient, nobody could make money simply by trading. The efficiency of markets is even more suspect, if one considers the cost of market making, from the cost of operating Wall Street investment banks and stock exchanges, to the cost of consumer behavior studies and television and internet advertising campaigns. Governments are probably not as effective as advocates claim. They have large bureaucracies that have their own interests; they are easy to corrupt; and they are not very responsive to changes in the environment. Evidence sited by each side is often selective and biased. Soviet Union's collapse is not reliable evidence of the superiority of the market system; any more than the rise of China is evidence of the superiority of government planning. There are many factors that influence the rise and fall of nations. So, it is probably more important to have a good government and high quality markets, rather than debating which is better. The critical debate should be not governments versus markets, but good government versus bad government, and efficient markets versus inefficient markets. But those debates are complex, and politically unattractive. In truth, the efficiency of markets and the effectiveness of governments are largely determined by the availability of various technologies that support them. Increasing availability of communication and information distribution technologies makes markets more efficient. Increasing availability of control and coordination technologies makes governments more efficient. The technological environment determines the correct mix, but the political debate is never that sophisticated [3, 6].

More insidiously, there are incentives to convince others that what serves your interests is also good for them. Controlling the thought processes of others is very valuable, because that leads to controlling their behavior. But the ability to convince others and control their behavior depends on what communication technologies are available, and how much control one has over them. That is why governments routinely limit access to public media, or limit what you can and cannot say over them. When governments cannot ban speech, they use businesses and social institutions to do the censoring for them by using economic and social pressures. There is a reason why we are constantly told to watch what we say on social media like Facebook or Twitter, because it might impact our job prospects; or to watch what we say at school or at work because it might impact our ability to work with others, or it might embarrass the institution. These are all techniques of censorship by using economic and social pressures to control our thoughts and beliefs. Both the censors and the censored use technology to increase their effectiveness. Monitoring technologies, from cameras and phone taps to email records and social media archives determine the effectiveness of censors. Information distribution technologies from cell phones and email to discussion boards and social media determine the effectiveness of the censored in distributing subversive ideas. Then, the control of such technologies becomes paramount to all involved. The control may be in the form of ownership and exclusive use; or it may be in the form of dominating and saturating a medium. Businesses, politicians, or celebrities often try to saturate the media with their messages, to drown out the competitive messages. This is why money is critical in politics, advertising, entertainment, and celebrity making. Once a monopoly is established over a medium you rely on, politicians can control your votes; businesses can control your purchases; celebrities can control your concepts of beauty, fashion, and love, and religious leaders can control your understanding of proper behavior. It was widely reported that a single concert by teenage idol Britney Spears established the belly-exposing shirts as the fashion for a whole generation of teenage girls. Mass communication technologies, and their ownership, are critical to this exercise of power. Decentralization of communication technologies, like the government-developed internet, is likely to change this power dynamic, compared to the privately owned and controlled technologies such as newspapers, radio and television stations, cable distribution systems, and movie studios [10, 20].

CHAPTER 6
FLEXIBLE AND DIVERSE INSTITUTIONS

Technology determines our knowledge, our values, and our beliefs. As technologies change, our beliefs and values change accordingly. But the change is chaotic and unpredictable with long delays and serious conflict. Change is inherently difficult because of the uncertainty it creates, but social institutions make it even more difficult since they are expressly created to maintain stability in values and beliefs, and hence resist change. Maintaining stability and predictability is important in human societies, but in a fast-changing technology-laden environment, stability and predictability increasingly become liabilities, as the institutions cannot adapt and become increasingly obsolete and maladaptive. Moreover, social institutions may resist change for more insidious reasons, such as to protect their constituencies, to cater to powerful groups, or even to maintain their own bureaucracies [25].

There are two fundamental solutions to such dysfunctional institutions. One is to increase their flexibility so that they can adjust to the changing environment faster, more efficiently, and with less conflict. Second is to create a diversity of social institutions that compete with each other, and to prevent the monopolization of social life by specific institutions. The two solutions are not independent, and may in fact be complementary, since competition may force institutions to become more flexible, and flexibility may make them more competitive.

Social institutions are critical to social organization and stability. Governments, businesses, markets, military, schools, hospitals, families, and churches are all complex institutions, designed to provide a multitude of services to their constituencies, through an elaborate system of social organization. They employ permanent bureaucracies to provide stability and reliability in the creation and delivery of those services. Yet, the stability they aim to provide makes them inflexible, and in a rapidly changing technology-laden environment, leads to obsolescence at an increasing rate. The dichotomy between stability and flexibility has been an enduring debate among social scientists. The classic problem of choosing between buying and leasing of resources in economics, the long standing controversy between government and business in political science, and the unending debate between markets and hierarchies in organizational sociology are all examples of this dichotomy. In all of these dichotomies, both solutions have advantages and disadvantages, leading to protracted philosophical debates on how to evaluate those advantages and disadvantages. But recently, new information technologies created new possibilities to resolve these long standing conflicts in creative ways, by eliminating the rigid rules that govern these institutions with respect to the ownership of resources, membership in institutions, and permanent bureaucracies [3, 43].

It is now possible to have an ownership mechanism for resources that is not absolute, where institution and even individuals can share resources with others, and have limited rights over resources to produce specific services, as opposed to unlimited rights of usage that comes with traditional ownership. But such limited and task specific ownership requires an infrastructure of monitoring and tracking technologies. It is now possible to have a membership mechanism that is not absolute, where members can belong to many competing institutions partially or conditionally. They would have limited rights and responsibilities within each institution, and can change their commitments dynamically and partially, as opposed to long-term, fixed, and total commitments that are typical now. But such fluid and dynamic memberships would require an infrastructure of electronic record keeping and data exchange technologies between these institutions. It is now possible to have institutional bureaucracies and management that are not fixed and permanent, but flexible and dynamic. They would be constituted from existing organizational components, from both inside and outside the organization. They would be created at the time of need and only to generate specific services, or to deal with specific threats or opportunities. They would be dissolved into their basic components immediately after the services are delivered or the specific projects are accomplished. These structures are typically called virtual organizations, and they require an infrastructure of coordination technologies such as electronic services, organizational ontologies and rich semantic descriptions, and modular design. All of these technologies are in their infancy, but they are essential to build flexible institutions where ownership, membership, and management are fluid, conditional, partial, and flexible [12, 24, 26].

Similarly, the existence of a diversity of institutions, with many alternatives to each institution, is critical in a fast changing society, with relatively free entry into and exit from each institution, to force them to complete for members. Businesses are not allowed to monopolize their markets, because it is widely accepted that monopolies perpetuate their power, and serve their own narrow constituencies, rather than the social interest. Yet, social institutions such as the state, military, church, family, and university are often allowed to monopolize their niches. They all require commitments that make it difficult for their members to switch loyalties; and they all try to undermine rival institutions from flourishing through a variety of social, political and legal arrangements. For example, no state allows free entry and exit through its national borders, so nation states provide an extreme example of a rigid and all-encompassing institution. Those who disagree with their nation on important matters rarely have the option to leave without major sacrifices, but they are forced to challenge their state and attempt to change it through political or even military conflict. Other institutions also have tendencies to block easy entry and exit, and demand that their members either be compliant, or face costly and prolonged conflict. For example, a family is a difficult social union to dissolve, and often requires lengthy and expensive court proceedings, especially when there are children and considerable assets involved. Even universities often make it difficult for students to transfer to other institutions without penalties. They certainly have severe restrictions when students try to mix and match offerings from multiple universities [20, 31, 38].

To solve these problems, and allow for a diversity of competing institutions, it would be useful to create super-institutions that are aggregates of institutions that compete with each other within a framework established by the super-institution. European Union may be a budding example of a super-institution, of multiple nation-states, where citizens are able to migrate between nations, and the nations compete with each other for the approval of the citizenry. Online marketplaces like Amazon is another example of a super-institution, where member businesses can set up shop within the Amazon framework and compete with each other. Yet Amazon sets up the framework of competition, and requires member businesses to follow certain guidelines and deploy compatible information systems, so that their business customers can easily establish business-to-business relationships with any of them, and also easily switch from one to another. This arrangement prevents exclusive and binding contracts that often inextricably tie small businesses to their larger partners. Similar arrangements can be useful where universities can encourage their students to enroll in multiple institutions and take advantage of offerings from all of them simultaneously; or where multiple families can form super-families and share child care, house-keeping, home maintenance, or even transportation and food preparation tasks. A modern coordination technology infrastructure would be essential for any of these super-institutions to be viable. That infrastructure would include ubiquitous networks for communication, electronic record keeping and electronic data interchange for coordination, sensor networks and tracking devices for monitoring resources, and electronic services to facilitate wide-spread sharing. They would also require major cultural shifts to be generally acceptable and widely adopted [21, 22, 27].

PART 2

PRIVACY, TRANSPARENCY AND IDENTITY AS TECHNOLOGICAL CONSTRUCTS

God can see everything, but you can never see God. That is the perfect design for control.

Privacy is a modern concern. It is a consequence of technologies that made it increasingly easier to track, monitor, and control others' information. The ability to access others' information while hiding your own is a significant source of power that is not always appreciated. This chapter demonstrates the critical importance of that power with a variety of examples ranging from ancient tribes to modern corporations, prisons to cults, and social movements to terrorist cells. The examples show how the technologies of intrusion and the technologies of protection led to the modern arms race between privacy and transparency. Paradoxically, increasing transparency is suggested as a solution to the modern privacy crisis.

CHAPTER 7
PRIVACY

Privacy is the ability to protect your information from others. Attacks on privacy are attempts to discover and extract others' information. Information is power, and hence both the ability to hide your information and the ability to discover others' information are sources of power. Both capabilities are highly dependent on available information technologies and the access to and the ownership of those technologies. As a result, privacy becomes a technological arms race between the technologies of information discovery, and the technologies of information protection. This arms race is the reason for increasing prominence of privacy as a modern social problem.

Consider your demographic information, such as your age, gender, income, and marital status. That information is useful to those who are selling various goods and services, and are anxious to locate potential customers of those products and services, and reach them with a convincing message to buy their products. As useful as it is, such demographic information used to be very difficult to utilize, since once you identify a potential customer, and create an appropriate message, then you would have to send a salesman to deliver the message. With the invention of telephone and later email, the cost of delivering such targeted messages dropped precipitously, and telemarketing and spam email were born. Simultaneously, the need to hide your demographic information came to prominence, to protect yourself from businesses that might target you. The age of obsession with privacy had arrived! And that privacy itself can only be achieved by using a variety of privacy protection technologies ranging from "do not call" lists and caller id's, to spam filters and fake online identities. A privacy arms race ensued, which continues ferociously to this day.

There is some confusion as to why the personalized messages of telemarketers and email marketers are harmful to the recipients of those messages. After all, if the message is targeted, it should be more useful than a mass distributed message. There are two reasons: First, there is a difference between targeting a consumer to serve his interests, and targeting him to take advantage of his weaknesses. If the consumer is a student, and the message is about cheap Spring Break travel; that may be useful to him. But if the consumer is a gambling addict and the message is about sweepstakes and lotteries; that may not be in his best interest. It is worse when the message is misleading. A message targeting teenagers and suggesting that drinking a brand of soda will make them popular, or smoking cigarettes will make them cool, or a message targeting middle aged men and suggesting that buying a sports car will make them sexually desirable to young women, or a message targeting elderly and suggesting that buying life insurance will make them worthwhile parents are misleading and manipulative of the emotional needs of consumers. Most commercial messages fall into this category. After all, advertising, relying on businesses to provide reliable information about their own products, is a faulty model. Businesses have an incentive and the means to distort product information in favor of their own products; and competition among multiple products, each with its own distorted message, does not necessarily add up to a correct and undistorted message [25].

Second, targeted messages such as telemarketing calls and spam email are universally despised because they involve the theft of a valuable resource, namely the time and attention of the recipient, without remuneration. Time and attention are valuable commodities, and you can actually sell your time and attention; but only if you can claim ownership to them and protect that ownership; and that requires privacy. Some retailers for example, give you shopping cards, in exchange for your name and address, and an opportunity to send you targeted messages; but in exchange they give you discounts on your purchases. Television and newspaper ads take your time and attention, but they give you news and entertainment in exchange. These are all examples of payments for your time and attention. Telemarketers and email marketers often take your time and attention without payment, because phone and email technologies took away the privacy of consumers against such intrusions.

Potential theft of property is the most common reason given for the need for privacy. After all, keeping your credit card number private prevents its theft and unauthorized use. Keeping your income and home address private protects you from being targeted for burglary. Technologies made such threats more serious. Large databases of credit card numbers, or employee addresses and incomes can be stolen to provide much higher returns and incentives to criminals than the theft of individual information.

But, direct theft of resources is just the beginning of the story. Privacy is effective in preventing discrimination by powerful economic, political, and social forces, which may be even more profitable and effective than direct theft, and can be done legally. Consider health records. If they are not kept private, employers and insurance companies can discriminate against those with current or potential health problems, if the law allows it. Privacy has economic value. If your sex life is not kept private, friends and colleagues can discriminate against you. It can be devastating to a teenage girl to be called a "slut" by her friends and peers. Privacy has social and psychological value. If your personal and religious life is not kept private, your colleagues and coworkers can discriminate against you. No atheist or adulterer is likely to make it to a high political office, as a large number of his constituents will discriminate against him. Privacy has strategic value [9].

These are not just theoretical concerns. Businesses, friends, and colleagues go to great lengths to invade your privacy and discover your personal secrets to gain an advantage over you, or to enforce social rules. And when they discover usable information, they often use it quite forcefully. Consider People's Express, the first discount airline in 1980's. It served only major cities, with no frills and completely full airplanes, and with fares well below the major airlines. It was a huge success and threatened the profitability or even the survival of all major airlines. Then, a new technology was introduced by American Airlines, called airline reservation systems, which destroyed People's Express' business model very quickly. Airline Reservation Systems exposed some information about customers that was heretofore private. The value each customer places on an airline ticket is different: a retired senior citizen visiting Grand Canyon and a business executive meeting a client place very different values on the same ticket. If the airlines could determine that value, they could charge a different price for the same ticket depending on who the customer is and how much he is willing to pay. Airline reservation systems revealed enough information about travelers to estimate that value, from their age, location, date and time of travel, date and time of purchase, and duration of stay. American Airlines was suddenly in a position to match Peoples Express' low prices for students and senior citizens, while charging a much higher fare to business executives. People's Express could not distinguish between the two groups, and had to charge the same fare, and consequently went bankrupt very quickly [22].

Businesses go to extreme lengths to price discriminate because it is very lucrative, as long as technologies enable them to break through customers' privacy. In 1800's in England, railroad technology created such opportunities. Railroad companies were cruel to 3rd class passengers, in these early days of railroads. Some 3rd class cars did not even have roofs; the passengers sat in the rain and snow unprotected. The railroad companies did not think that was enough punishment, so they put the 3rd class cars in front of the train, right behind the engine, so the passengers sat in the smoke, and burned their hair in the amber, from the dirty and smoky engines of early railroads. Why did they hate the 3rd class passengers so much? Actually they didn't! They simply wanted to make sure that nobody would be tempted to travel cheaply in the 3rd class, unless they were absolutely dirt poor, and couldn't possibly afford the 2nd class fare. It was a trick to extract the information about their willingness to pay, in the absence of modern technologies that pierce customer privacy much more effectively. Modern airlines are increasingly adopting the same trick as they make coach seats increasingly uncomfortable, crowded, and restrictive, even to the extent of charging extra for an aisle seat, or extra suitcase. Such price discrimination can be done much more effectively, even without the explicit knowledge of the customer, by using the vast online repositories of World Wide Web, Search Engines, and Social Networks. Technologies determine the ability of businesses to collect information, to bypass privacy protections of their customers, and to use price discrimination to their economic advantage [18, 23].

Social discrimination is even more subtle. Humans are social animals and need emotional support from, and bonding with, other humans. We need to belong to a group for our emotional well-being, and that makes us vulnerable to the group, and also gives us the power to build alliances against our adversaries. Social acceptance is a fundamental social need for humans, and privacy protects us from the power of our social group. Social group is a cohesive unit that communicates regularly through social events, enforces the group rules, and punishes the rule breakers to maintain group identity. Most social conversation is utterances that reinforce group cohesion without any particular substance to what is being said, sometimes called "small talk". Gossip is a very effective tool that tracks the group members by penetrating their privacy, and identifies and punishes rule breakers, by isolating them and even pushing them out of the group. Bullying is also a technique in establishing group solidarity both by defining the group and the outsider, but also by punishing the outsider. Social networks have adapted all these techniques to the electronic media without any significant change [7, 12].

Political and employment discrimination goes a step beyond social discrimination, and involves institutions such as corporations, government agencies, military, universities, and political parties. All such institutions have codes of conduct that often involves private behavior such as sex, gambling, or alcohol and drug use. A New York Congressman, Anthony Wiener, was forced to resign in 2011, for engaging in cybersex. In a clear confusion of online private behavior with public behavior, congressional leaders likened cybersex to public nudity and indecent exposure. In fact, private behavior online is more like private behavior at home, as it is private. If the other party chooses to reveal such private behavior, it would be ignored if it was at one's home, but it is publicized and ostracized if it is online. Clearly, online privacy is critically important to those in public eye, since the public doesn't seem to accept it as similar to privacy at home [32].

Similarly, Senator Craig of Idaho was admonished for alleged lewd behavior for soliciting gay sex in a public bathroom in 2007. Leaving aside the legal issues, a primary concern of his constituents was hypocrisy, since he was a vocal critic of the gay lifestyle. There are two problems with the hypocrisy argument: First, if he was a good senator before his private life was exposed, presumably if he had privacy, he would have continued to serve his constituents competently, including his anti-gay constituents. Just because he may have had homosexual tendencies in private, does not make him less competent. Hypocrisy is a strange argument, because it insists on complete knowledge of a public servant's private life, and complete consistency of his private life with his public advocacy. It seems to be an unnecessarily stringent requirement, not essential for competence. Second, there seems to be some confusion between interest in homosexual activity, and subscribing to a gay lifestyle. They are two different things. One can have one without the other. One is private behavior; the other is a public pronouncement and advocacy. Many ancient cultures, such as ancient Greeks, accepted homosexual behavior, even with children, but were not tolerant of a homosexual lifestyle. They expected everybody to have families and children, yet engage in homosexual activity on the side, without advocating it as a permanent and exclusive lifestyle. Similarly, Iranian president was widely ridiculed in a lecture at Columbia University in 2010, when he declared: "we do not have gays in Iran the way you do in the US". In fact, he is probably right that they do not have a public gay lifestyle in Iran the way we do in the United States, probably because of repression and cultural reasons. They certainly have homosexual activity, but that is very different from a public gay lifestyle. A quick review of ads for men seeking men on Craigslist shows that most of the ads are by heterosexual men with families, looking for an easy and quick sexual adventure, and they have no interest in a gay lifestyle. Privacy keeps such proclivities out of the public eye, and irrelevant to their public lifestyle. Lack of privacy would unnecessarily elevate all such activity to the level of a lifestyle. It is ironic that some who advocate privacy rights also demand no hypocrisy. Privacy is important precisely because it allows some level of hypocrisy, by separating our private lives from our public posture [3, 33].

CHAPTER 8
CONTROL AND IDENTITY

Control is the evil twin of privacy, because when you have no privacy, your information is often controlled by others. Privacy protects us from such information control. Otherwise, powerful interests could bombard us with large amounts of information, and block our ability to choose our information sources, evaluate them, and make intelligent decisions. Humans have limited ability to process information, and when they are overloaded, they resort to heuristics and shortcuts, or in more extreme cases, randomly discard information, to make the task of information processing more manageable. Television advertising has this effect. It is almost impossible for a television viewer to assess and evaluate all the commercial messages she sees in a 1-hour television program, and make intelligent decisions about them. As a result, viewers resort to intuitive shortcuts to process them very quickly. Advertisers take advantage of this, by providing easy to process, intuitive, and often subliminal shortcuts to the actual message. The shortcuts are often misleading, and have no pretense of being substantive. A soda commercial may have beautiful and popular teenagers, although the beverage company would not explicitly claim that drinking their soda will make you a beautiful and popular teenager. A car commercial may have beautiful women admiring their cars in sexually suggestive poses, although the car company will not explicitly claim that owning their cars will make you attractive to sexually available beautiful women. Such messages are designed to penetrate our defenses against an avalanche of information. Politicians also take advantage of this weakness in human information processing, and convert complex issues to easy, intuitive, short sound bites. Once the messages are simplified to overcome our defenses, all one has to do is to overload the viewers, so that they can't process them, and accept the simple, easy to digest messages as given. Privacy of viewers can protect them from this onslaught, if they can set complex criteria about what types of messages they would like to receive; then they would have the time and the intellectual resources to evaluate those few messages correctly. Privacy requires an effective filtering technology to protect the recipients of commercial and political messages from an information overload [2, 13].

Controlling what information people receive is an important source of power. We are often told we are what we eat; but more importantly, we are what we learn; and what we learn is determined by what information we receive. Our identity, our values, and our life's goals, are determined by what we learn. In extreme cases, complete control of someone's information sources can provide complete control of their identity and self-perception. Cults use this power very effectively. When you join a cult, the very first thing they do is to take away your privacy. You are never alone; and they control all of your information intake, by isolating you from other information sources. In that environment, in very short order, you lose your individuality, and acquire the group identity. Patti Hearst, the daughter of the famous Hearst publishing magnate, was kidnapped in 1974 by a domestic terrorist group called Symbionese Liberation Army, and within a short time she identified with the objectives of the group's political ideology, and started participating in their armed robberies and violent confrontations with the police. Kidnapping victims often identify with their captors. It is called Stockholm syndrome. They may even fall in love with their kidnappers. A 14 year old Salt Lake City girl, Elizabeth Smart, was kidnapped from her home in 2002 by a couple, and she was taken as a second wife by the kidnappers. She reportedly identified with her kidnappers, so although she was not guarded and travelled extensively with her kidnappers publicly, she never attempted to escape. When she was located and rescued, she had to be deprogrammed, like many ex-cult members, to change her attitude towards her captors. Lack of privacy and control can completely alter one's identity and self-perception. Military uses similar techniques, to a lesser extent, to create a team spirit and a group identity, by separating the recruits from their natural environment, and denying some privacy by forcing them to be with each other continuously, to the exclusion of all non-military personnel. This creates a strong group identity; and soldiers often reminisce fondly of the unparalleled group cohesion they experienced in military. Similar, albeit lesser, effects can be seen in university fraternities, sororities, and dormitories [28].

If it is so easy to be programmed, reprogrammed and deprogrammed, we should be very skeptical of our concepts of self-determination and rational decision making. In fact, we are what we are taught! Starting with parents and teachers, and continuing with public media, books, movies, tv programs, celebrities, and sports figures, there is a constant effort to shape our thoughts and values. Privacy allows us to pick and choose, and gives us a modicum of control. With no privacy, we would be at the mercy of whoever controls our information. If there are no explicit controls, information overload often leads to the loudest and most intrusive voices winning our mind. This is especially true with commercial and political messages.

It is no coincidence that political campaigns are getting increasingly expensive, and politicians are increasingly preoccupied with fund raising, because money allows one to dominate the information sources and control the voters' information. In effect, our democracy has been converted from "one man one vote" to "one dollar one vote". Commercial messages are equally expensive to distribute. Advertising budgets of major corporations are obscenely high, and they increasingly dominate the information sources of their consumers, both against their smaller competitors, but also against apathy. The most critical issue for a corporation is for the consumers to ignore your product, or to despise it. So, in their effort to compete with each other, all businesses in an industry actually reinforce each other's messages to overcome the apathy of consumers towards their products collectively. The counter message against a whole class of products often does not exist, fueling the consumer society. For example, all soda companies push their own sodas as the best; but there is no commercial interest pushing the message against all sodas! Consequently, soda drinking becomes the norm [2, 13].

Privacy protects us against such assaults on our information sources, but it is very difficult to achieve that level of privacy where you can filter messages before they arrive at you, rather than being forced to process them before you can discard them. An effective privacy regime requires a filtering system that protects you from exposure to unwanted messages in the first place, rather than forcing you to process them. Because the very act of processing them, exposes you to subliminal messages, overwhelms you with information overload and forces you to use simple heuristics which makes you vulnerable to manipulation, blocks out the messages you would like to receive by dominating your limited time and attention, and takes away your time and attention without any remuneration.

Privacy also has a dark side. It often isolates us from a permanent community and fixed values. That can lead to a fragmented identity, and loneliness. People who move from a traditional rural society where the extended family has a permanent and complete hold on the individual, to a modern urban society where the individual is physically separated from the extended family and has access to a variety of information sources and value systems, often pick and choose and even mix and match from a variety of lifestyles. That often leads to a fragmented identity where the individual identifies with a variety of disparate groups, lifestyles and values for different objectives. Lack of a permanent identity group leads to loneliness, a modern affliction, because humans are social animals and have a need to belong to a permanent and fixed group of about 20, just like other primates. People often look back at their military and college days with great fondness when they had a group to belong, which often indoctrinated them and somewhat isolated them from outside influences. Tribal societies often have permanent and geographically fixed groups with little autonomy or privacy for the individual. They look oppressive to our modern eyes, but they are often very harmonious societies with little crime and internal conflict; and the concept of loneliness is often foreign to them. In some tribal societies where the individual has no access to the outside world, and the tribe acts as a single unit in all endeavors from food and shelter to sex and child rearing, and from warfare and law to religion and medicine, the individual identity can be completely lost and replaced with a tribal identity [15, 24].

Modern life on the other hand requires us to play many roles, isolated from each other, and creates a fragmented identity. Professional work is all about creating an artificial identity isolated from the personal identity, and playing the role required by that identity, unaffected by any personal attachment.

Professional code of conduct requires leaving personal concerns and attachments outside the professional realm, and often demands wearing a uniform signifying that personal concerns have been left behind. That is why surgeons do not like to operate on their own family members; prostitutes do not like to have sex with personal friends and family; teachers do not like to have their own kids in their classes; soldiers do not like to fight alongside their spouses, and nobody likes to take a shower with their professional colleagues. Dress codes often serve to signify this separation between the personal and professional life, ranging from suits for businessmen and white coats and scrubs for doctors and nurses, to miniskirts for prostitutes and fatigues for soldiers. That is a sharp contrast to earlier human societies where attachments were permanent and all encompassing.

There is considerable evidence that technologies that created the modern lifestyles with fragmented identities also created various mental illnesses that involve fragmented identities. Industrial revolution led to a breakdown of communities formed around crafts and small scale agriculture, often based on extended family ties. The elimination of such permanent communities was necessary since the new large scale industrial operations required each individual to specialize, and also to move wherever they are needed. That led to an individualistic lifestyle with no permanent and stable anchors, where every individual was judged by its own performance rather than assuming a group identity and performing as a group. Every person now had to define himself, set his own life goals, choose his own community, and be responsible for his own happiness. That was revolutionary. And it led to some unexpected consequences. People suddenly started developing new types of mental illnesses in great numbers that involved fragmented personalities. Schizophrenia rates skyrocketed in England where the industrial revolution first emerged, so much so that it was called "The English Malady". The new diseases spread to the rest of the world, along with the spread of new industrial technologies and the new lifestyles they brought about. In addition, a number of other less serious psychological maladies such as "loneliness" and "depression" became major epidemics, although they used to be rare in earlier tribe, clan, or extended family based societies [11].

Can we have privacy and control over our information sources, yet have a group identity to meet our emotional needs? This is a modern dilemma. Modern societies try to solve this dilemma by creating artificial communities around hobbies, sports teams, political parties, colleges, and even nations, but they don't have the intimacy and cohesion of a small permanent group. Even so, it is telling how emotionally attached people become to some of these artificial communities such as sports teams or political parties, even to describe their identity partially in terms of them. Popularity of online social networks is also a testament to this need. Social Networks have the potential to alleviate this problem, if they can extend their reach from purely online exchanges of pictures and gossip, to real world communities with shared responsibilities such as group living and child rearing, group education and cooperative careers, community business ventures and financial commitments. Those would lead to online support for communities with emotional substance and enforced commitment.

CHAPTER 9
CRIME AND PUNISHMENT

George Orwell once said that a prison is the only place where you can consistently find interesting people who defy conventional wisdom and think for themselves. People with unconventional ideas and lifestyles often find themselves in prison, especially in autocratic societies. However, once in prison, it is difficult to have an unconventional lifestyle, since the prison takes away privacy and control necessary for it. Without adequate privacy, it is very difficult to have non-conforming behavior, or even a separate identity from the group. In or out of a prison, if everything is visible and transparent, powerful groups will dictate all acceptable behavior, by making non-conforming behavior socially unacceptable, or even illegal. They will use the power of social pressure through embarrassment, exclusion, and ridicule, or use the force of law to incarcerate, exile, or even kill. The resistance to such social and legal pressure is very difficult, as readily evidenced in overcoming the bullying epidemic in high schools, in resisting the strict sexual mores of the traditional societies, or fighting the political oppression in class-based or autocratic societies. Any teenager who was called a "slut" or "sissy", or any adult who was called a "pervert" or "lowlife" knows the power of social pressure, and the difficulty of overcoming it, even when legal force is not used. Privacy protects us from such pressure [14].

Is there an incentive to exercise such power? Why won't we let people be? The powerful groups benefit from the exercise of power, or conversely, power not exercised does not exist. Consider polygamist cults like FLDS in Utah. Cult leaders, like Warren Jeffs, often exercise power by delivering and withholding sexual privileges. Sex is a fundamental human need, and anyone who controls it has tremendous power over others. Polygamist cult leaders punish disobedient men by limiting their access to wives, or denying them a wife altogether. They reward obedience with very young brides, often considered the most desirable, and with many of them. This is a very effective reward and punishment system. In an environment where there is no sexual privacy, the leader controls who has access to how much sex and with whom. Cults achieve this power by eliminating all sexual privacy; otherwise the members would bypass the restrictions. Mainstream religions also exercise similar control over sex, by insisting that sex is limited to marriage, and requiring that marriages are performed by the church. Cults also limit the members' interaction with outsiders, and control their access to outside information; otherwise members would have the option to compare and contrast, reject the rules they don't like, and seek sex elsewhere [28, 33].

Religion in general is a powerful tool to limit privacy, and exercise control. European missionaries used religion brilliantly to control indigenous people in Africa. In explaining the economic function of missionaries in Africa, Bishop Desmond Tutu of South Africa said: "When missionaries came, they had the Bible and we had the land, when they were done, we had the Bible and they had the land". Religions often deliver and control information about the fundamental goals and values of human life, and that is a great source of power. Missionaries were critical in diverting the information sources of natives from local leaders and indigenous religions to the colonial leaders and European religions. If the natives are receiving their information about the fundamental goals and values of life from you, then you can direct them into behaviors that serve your economic and political interests, such as donating some of their income to your church, paying taxes to your administrative bureaucracy, opening their lands to your industrial development, and fighting your wars against those who resist your economic interests. Some religions are especially effective in political control, because they threaten eternal damnation, punishment that continues even after death; and they enforce their rules with an all-seeing and all-knowing god. That leaves no room for even a modicum of privacy, hence no individual freedom at all. When information control is that effective, punishment is not even necessary [1].

Where religion fails, autocratic regimes take over. They watch their people relentlessly, and punish any dissent forcefully. They accomplish this with extensive police and military force, but more importantly, with peer-watching, peer-reporting, and peer-punishment systems. Short of an all-seeing and all-knowing god, an all-encompassing peer-watching system is the next best thing. Such lack of privacy is critical to catching dissent early, before it spreads and becomes difficult to suppress. As one would expect, the other component of an autocratic system is the control of information sources of citizens, with constant distortion of the information they receive to control their behavior into compliance with the interests of powerful rulers. Lack of privacy prevents dissenters from advocating and disseminating dangerous ideas; control over their information prevents them from learning about and acquiring the dangerous ideas in the first place. Together, they fuel autocratic regimes [9].

Modern democratic societies also use similar techniques. Powerful political groups have an incentive to control information sources like newspapers, television stations, movies, and educational institutions. They also watch and suppress dangerous ideas thorough social, economic, and legal pressure. Most corporations and social institutions have codes of behavior for their employees that often include their private behavior outside of the workplace. Violations can lead to dismissal; and employees may not have much of privacy protection, since the courts ruled repeatedly that employees have no privacy rights when communicating over employer owned communication devices, even if the behavior is private. Corporations also often rely on peer complaints to punish private behavior of employees if that behavior is embarrassing to the company. Social Networks have made such peer-watching much more effective. Any posting by an employee of a major company has to carefully navigate social norms about acceptable private behavior, ranging from sexual and alcohol related postings to embarrassing office gossip or criticism of corporate policies or even personalities of bosses. Any behavior that crosses an invisible social red line can lead to dismissal, which puts private enterprises in the business of enforcing social rules about private behavior through economic pressure. It is no wonder that young people are constantly warned about watching what they put on their Facebook pages. After all, big brother is always watching, indirectly through a million vigilante eyes of your peers [9, 14].

Civil strife and war amplifies the efforts to control. All parties try to spin the facts, and engage in an information war; and all parties try to discredit those who hold subversive ideas. During the Cold War, the US engaged in an information war through Voice of America radio stations to disseminate information about the Western values and the virtues of capitalism and Western style democracy. At the same time, there was a concerted effort to identify domestic communist sympathizers and suppress their advocacy with ridicule, embarrassment, denial of employment, and even prison if a criminal charge such as being a foreign agent could be mustered [17].

The end of war doesn't end the information war. Winners always write the history, and try to portray the losers as evil and inhuman, and deserving their fate, justifying the winners' actions. If Germany had won World War 2, there is no doubt that history books would be full of American and British atrocities against civilians in the bombings of Dresden or Hiroshima, or the suffering of the interned Japanese in American concentration camps. The stories would likely be similar to the stories of suffering in European concentration camps, since if America had lost the war, and faced an all-out invasion, starvation, and disease, Japanese interns would probably have suffered a similarly horrifying fate involving a great deal of disease, violence, and death. Putting people in concentration camps unleashes a series of events one may have never planned. The technology of identifying and isolating people from the general population has serious psychological and physical consequences for the interned. This is how modern prisons operate also [8].

All governments operate in relative secrecy, some more than others, because governments are rarely purely representative of all the people, but they often represent powerful economic interests at the expense of the masses. They can maintain the illusion of populism by their privacy and secrecy, and by controlling the information received by the masses. Transparency can expose that fact and endanger their legitimacy. That is why WikiLeaks is such a threat to governments and corporations all over the world. It encourages insiders to reveal government and corporate secrets, and it publishes them unedited on its web site. Not only it promotes complete transparency, but it also relies on an independent and unedited medium, World Wide Web, to deliver its messages. In fact,

WikiLeaks is the epitome of the original goal of the World Wide Web, all the world's information, from all sources, completely unedited and uncontrolled [29]. Early World Wide Web was symbol of free and uncontrolled expression, combined with complete privacy, probably a first in human history. With no commercial activity, and no government controls, it flourished with content that would have been suppressed in the larger society. The early content ranged from sublime to bizarre, ordinary to violent, sexual to religious, innocent to daring. Anything and everything was on the web freely circulating to anyone who was curious and adventurous. It was not unusual to see children and adults, terrorists and mobsters, priests and academics, sex starved and the sex peddler, suicidal and the murderer, prostitutes and the pornographers, all mingling and exposing their most private thoughts and actions. It did not last long of course, but this kind of explosion of freedom happens with all new communication technologies. First to adopt are always the oppressed and the suppressed, who latch onto any new technology to break its bondage, out of desperation. Then come the commercial interests, with a considerable delay, because it takes a while to ensure enough security and trust to allow the exchange of goods and money. Finally, the government and the law enforcement move in, to regulate and control. There is further delay because they have to recognize the need to control, by observing a threat to the existing law and order, before they can dedicate the funds and the personnel to eradicate the threat. That means that with every new communication technology, first there is an opportunity for the outlawed and the suppressed to break free; then there is an opportunity to make money without government control and regulation. These opportunities, although short lived, can be significant, and can have long-lasting impact. VCR technology of 1980's is often credited with the rise of pornography, because it allowed viewing of pornography at the comfort of your home. WWW is blamed for the rise in child pornography because it allowed the private sharing of homemade movies. Mobile phones and social media have been credited with effective organization of terrorists and also mass democracy movements, because they allowed real-time coordination. Cameras on mobile phones led to citizen journalism, because they allowed real-time reporting by ordinary citizens with no journalistic editing and no government controls. Bypassing government and social controls can have a profound effect on social movements and social restrictions; because privacy empowers the powerless, the suppressed, and the criminal [4, 6].

Crime requires privacy to plan, develop, and recruit partners. That is why autocratic regimes often have little crime. But control suppresses dissent and alternative lifestyles, so it fosters lingering frustration. That is why there is a subtle balance between privacy and control. Too much privacy can lead to chaos and anarchy by allowing the individuals to follow their own interests; too much control can create unhappy and angry masses. This is the reason why punishment has to be proportional to the crime, not because of any moral principle. Too little punishment leaves the individuals free to flaunt the rules; too much punishment creates periodic and violent uprisings by the dissatisfied and the disenchanted. Consider the punishment for drug and sex crimes. In some countries, these crimes are punishable by death, because they are considered to be "murder of the soul". As expected, these countries have little of these crimes; but when they do occur, they are extremely violent, because of the pent up frustration with the harshness of the laws, and the expectation of heavy punishment anyway.

Punishment also has to consider the power and influence of the criminal. Otherwise, excessive punishment can trigger even more crime than before, since those influenced by the criminal can retaliate and seek revenge. Consider pickpocketing, a relatively minor crime in the modern world. In 1800's in England, it was considered a major crime, and repeat offenders were often sentenced to death by hanging. These executions were public spectacles, and large crowds showed up to watch them. They would bring their families and picnic baskets, and cheer the execution as if it was a sports event. One such event involved three executions in one afternoon, with an enthusiastic audience of about 800 people. During the three-hours of festivities celebrating the executions, twelve more people were pickpocketed! Why such a dramatic failure of such a severe punishment? To understand the reasons, one has to appreciate the social structure of 1800's England, where a permanent underclass resented the upper and merchant classes, and identified with the pickpockets. Harsh punishment only served to underlie the class struggle and reinforce the resentment [5]. Every punishment sends two clear messages to the society. One from the state which says "this is what happens to you if you do this crime". Those who are leading comfortable privileged lives hear that message clearly and rejoice. The second message is from the criminal which says "what I did was worth the punishment". The criminally inclined disadvantaged segments of the society hear the second message much more clearly, because they don't trust the state anyway, and they are often suicidal with their miserable lives, and punishment does not mean much to them.

In extreme cases, harsh punishment can lead to a full rebellion against the rules and the rulers. The execution of Prophet Jesus Christ by the Romans did precisely that, and led to a world-wide religious movement that devoured even the Roman Empire itself. Punishment then needs to be inversely proportional to the power of the criminal. Very powerful criminals such as political leaders, high-ranking soldiers, sex and drug criminals with whom others may sympathize, white collar criminals with powerful friends, are not punished severely because the punishment may backfire. The criminals with little power such as street criminals, low-ranking soldiers, destitute property criminals, mentally ill such as serial murderers, arsonists, and bizarre sex criminals like necrophiliacs, are punished severely because they and their supporters cannot easily retaliate.

Technology is critical in determining the power of the criminal. Communication technologies allow them to reach sympathizers and proselytize. Weapons technologies increase the power of all, including the criminal and the powerless, and bridge the power gap. The common wisdom in the Old West was that "the gun is the great equalizer". So are the modern explosives. Coupled with modern transportation technologies, they brought an end to colonialism in many parts of the world, and led to the rise of modern terrorism, which gave power to small disenfranchised groups at the expense of large powerful states. "Plastic explosives are the new great equalizers".

Historically, as new technologies increased the power of the criminal, the punishment changed from eliminating the criminal to controlling his message. When you capture a political leader, killing him does not end his political movement, especially if there is an organizational structure that maintains his support group and provides succession, and even encourages retaliation. There is a need then to be mindful of his power, to mete out punishment gingerly, and if possible to get him to change his political message explicitly or implicitly. Enter the concept of modern prison. Prison is a modern construct designed to take away the privacy, control the mind, and to shape his implicit message to others who identify with him, instead of physically eliminating him. Trials are theater, where the defendant is objectified, and is not even allowed to speak. The trial involves a ritualistic and sanitized discussion of the crime by respectable members of the community, and focuses narrowly on determining what acts were committed and what laws are applicable to those acts. The real issues of why the defendant acted the way he did, how we can prevent such acts in the future, who identifies with the criminal and finds the law unacceptable, and what the law should be are considered irrelevant to the trial. Even after conviction, the supporters are expected to ask for leniency, and the victims are expected to recite their grievances and their suffering. Questioning the system and challenging the process are never allowed. Finally, the criminal himself is encouraged or even coerced to apologize and show remorse, a clearly meaningless act if one is coerced to do it; yet it is critically important to shape the criminal's implicit message to the larger audience that is witnessing the theater of trial, may identify with the criminal, and may be influenced by him. It is important to send the right message, and punishment alone does not do it [8].

Prison itself is a show designed to objectify and dehumanize the criminal. Once upon a time, killing and torture were the common punishments. They modified the physical body of the criminal. Prisons modify the mind. At a time when people communicated with their physical presence and their body, killing and torture may have been effective, and many creative ways were invented to send the message forcefully. Serbian rulers, in the Middle Ages, perfected a technology where a long stick was inserted into the whole length of a criminal's body, from anus to mouth, but without killing him, and then he was exhibited to the general public in the town square with the stick in him for several days, as he slowly died. Roman crucifixion, Chinese water torture, European guillotines, and Middle Eastern amputations all had the same effect. The body was altered, objectified, torn to pieces, and eliminated [3].

As technologies changed, and people started communicating remotely, through writing and printing, and later by electronic communication, killing was not as effective, since the ideas continued to propagate. One has to control the mind to take away the power of ideas. Prisons are invented for this purpose, where the prisoners continue to communicate with the outside world, and try to prove that they changed their behavior, and they are remorseful. This is called rehabilitation. However, with ever increasing power of communication technologies, prisons may have lost their effectiveness to modify minds. Prison is a show for the outsiders, and as such the biggest danger is inmate defiance. But it is difficult to make prison a show, where outsiders can look in (no privacy), without insiders looking out (no control). Consequently, not having complete control of prisoners' information allows them to create a prison culture by importing some of their outside ideas into the prison. If prisoners can set the norms and enforce the rules of behavior, as opposed to the prison system and the guards, then a criminal culture is created inside the prison and forces everyone to conform. The prison becomes an institution of counterculture, a criminal education enterprise, with results quite contrary to its stated objectives [8].

The modern prison was invented by Jeremy Bentham in 1791. Prison as punishment, he called Panapticon, was a radical concept since previously prisons were mere temporary holding places before a trial or execution. In his design, prisoners are prevented from interacting with each other, by placing them in permanent solitary confinement, in cells placed around a circular courtyard. But they are always observed by the guards in a tower in the center of the courtyard. The observation tower had one-way glass so the prisoners could not even see the guards, but they were always under observation because their cell had a glass wall facing the courtyard. This design accomplished the objective of no privacy and complete control with the existing technologies of the time. Bentham's architecture was never implemented. But modern technologies of cameras and sensors make his dream of no privacy and complete control much more practical. Cameras are already being deployed in a large scale in urban areas and also in the phones of fellow citizens, to take away privacy. Sensors and sensor networks will take away the remaining privacy, by monitoring citizens even when they are away from cameras and other people. Modern urban life is also increasingly isolating physically, because of the mobility created by transportation technologies and global economies. As a result of mobility, and a lack of permanent group identification, our information intake is increasingly controlled by electronic media as opposed to face to face contact. Controlling those media would accomplish Bentham's dream of information control in a large scale. Bentham already suggested that this architecture was applicable, not just to prisons, but to all institutions such as the military, schools, hospitals, even families, where controlling people's minds in addition to their bodies was critical. But one has to be very careful, since with great power comes great responsibility. Humans are social animals, and need privacy and control over their information to have personal identities. There is evidence from monkey experiments that monkeys that are isolated, and strictly controlled, become anti -social and even schizophrenic in short order. In an effort to control the society, we always risk the danger of creating wide-spread mental illness. Already there are epidemics of depression, attention deficit disorder, and autism in the Western World; and our high-tech lifestyle with its physical isolation of the individual, electronic communication, and fragmented social life are suggested as possible culprits [24].

CHAPTER 10
POWER

Privacy and no-control are not essential to a well-functioning society, but they provide an insurance mechanism to protect the powerless from excessive exploitation by the powerful. Many ancient societies flourished with little or no privacy and extensive control of their members. Modern preoccupation with privacy and control arose primarily because modern communication technologies such as phones and internet that created opportunities to observe others surreptitiously; and because of modern information dissemination technologies such as newspapers, radio, and television that created opportunities to control others' information effectively. The obvious solution to such technological threats is to use defensive technologies to counter them, leading to a technological arms race. New technologies often create power differentials between those who own the technology and those who consume it. To remedy the power differential, a technological or organizational fix is sought by the disadvantaged. Excessive concentration of power almost always encourages a technological arms race to counter it, or creates social resistance movements to build new alliances to balance the power.

Great empires of the past often followed this trajectory of acquiring power by taking advantage of new technologies, but in the process encouraged their subjects to build alliances against the empire and seek technologies to bolster their resistance to the empire. Almost any attempt to grab power instigates a counter-attempt to resist it, and the resistance rises as the power increases. So one needs to be careful about the exercise of power, even when it produces immense advantages in the short term; and should contemplate the reaction to that exercise of power in the long term. Consider the British Empire. It was enabled by the warfare technologies of gunpowder, artillery, and gunships. Like all empires, it took advantage of technologies it owned, used them against those who didn't, to control and subjugate large populations of people over large swaths of land. And like all empires, it over extended itself by grabbing increasingly more power, as the short-term economic and political incentives dictate. Yet, every extension of power encouraged alliances against it, and spurred search for technologies to overcome the power imbalance. Alliances formed from India, Russia, and Afghanistan, to France, Spain, and the Americas, and as the technologies of artillery and gunships spread widely, they eroded the power of the Empire. Empires often follow this trajectory of rise with the new technology, and fall as the technology spreads, defensive technologies are developed, and alliances are formed to challenge the power imbalance. Resistance and social movements are critical to this process [19].

Privacy can be critically important to all social movements, not just armed resistance to empires, but wherever there is a power differential. It is important both to those trying to maintain the power differential, and to those trying to resist it. Consider why private behaviors such as sex and drug use are strictly regulated by social norms and even laws. If it is private behavior, why is there so much interest in controlling it? If it has public impact, why is there so much interest in hiding it? First, very few behaviors are purely private. Sex typically involves two people, and requires a search to find a suitable and willing partner. The search itself requires publicity to locate partners; and it requires education about the desirability and health consequences of various sex acts. That information itself is produced and distributed by others with a variety of interests of their own, and incentives to control and distort that information. Similarly, drugs are rarely produced, distributed, and consumed all by a single individual alone. Production requires skills and raw materials that need to be developed and procured; producers have to search for consumers and promote the product; and the consumers need to learn about the product, its desirability, its health effects, and how to use it properly. All of that information also needs to be produced and distributed by others with interests and incentives of their own. None of these activities are purely private behavior. Second, even if they were completely private acts, they threaten economic collusive agreements that benefit powerful groups. All prohibitions limit the supply of something. As such, they have economic consequences. Often, they constitute monopolistic behavior to control the price of a product, service, or information, and to keep it artificially high. Consider prostitution. Prohibition of prostitution limits the availability of cheap sex, which forces the price of sex higher. Price of sex in traditional relationships involve a variety of payments by men, in the form of gifts, dinners, engagement rings, financial and emotional commitments as in marriage, child support and child rearing, and alimony after a divorce. Prostitution does not involve any of those payments. There is a reason why prostitutes are called "cheap", or they are said to "cheapen" women's value. Those are true statements in the economic sense of "cheap". Polls show that housewives widely detest prostitution, and favor its prohibition, probably because it is a cheap alternative to their economic livelihood. Professional women on the other hand largely support its decriminalization, probably because it does not threaten their economic livelihood. And there may be a psychological identification with them, after all prostitutes were the first "professional" women. Technologies often create cheap alternatives to existing services, and powerful interest groups move to discourage them socially or prohibit them legally. Birth control and disease control technologies made prostitution possible in a large-scale, and increasingly safe and readily available to the mainstream public. More recently, communication technologies such as online communities and specialized web sites allowed people to engage in prostitution on a part-time basis, without intermediation. A variety of web sites dedicated to finding mistresses, wealthy dates, sugar babies, or friends with benefits are changing the nature of prostitution, and even the nature of mainstream male-female relationships, by making the value exchange and payments explicit [30, 33].

Consider marijuana smoking. Is it a private activity with no impact on others? It certainly has an impact on competitive products and activities that are more expensive. One reason why marijuana was made illegal in the first place was the intense lobbying by the competing industries such as alcohol as a drug, and oil-based plastics competing against plant-based hemp plastics. Marijuana was a threat to those industries as a cheap alternative, since anybody could grow it easily. Also, marijuana was a cheap drug, mainly for lower classes, and it was affecting their availability as labor. The business interests prefer lower classes as married with kids and financial responsibilities, so that they would increase labor supply and depress labor costs. Marijuana on the other hand, like opium before it, kept the potential labor high and happy, and not available for strenuous labor at low prices. Technologies often create cheaper alternatives to drugs, or even states of mind like happiness, and threaten powerful interests that depend on alternative products and states of mind [20].

Consider gay rights. Prohibitions against homosexual activity may have started because of the need for reproduction and the need for population increase in militaristic and agricultural societies. But it reached a feverish pitch as the marriage institution changed from a purely economic arrangement between extended families to an economic bond between two people with an emotional overlay. Such a fragile emotional bond was threatened by any other emotional bonds, whether it is adultery or homosexual adventures by otherwise heterosexual men. Homosexual activity was especially threatening because it involved less financial commitment, since no reproduction was involved, and as such it was a cheaper alternative. The threat was primarily heterosexual men engaging in homosexual activity on the side. To this day, a quick review of matching sites reveals that most of homosexual activity involves otherwise heterosexual men looking for cheap and easy sexual adventures. That is threatening to traditional families. It is no surprise then housewives overwhelmingly oppose expanding gay rights, and professional women overwhelmingly support them. Women's rights movement has been especially supportive of gay rights, seen as an ally in challenging the patriarchy, but even more importantly as a natural ally in their struggle against the traditional family roles. Women's movement itself was a technology-inspired movement. Household technologies such as indoor plumbing and electric appliances automated housework, and the interest in large families dwindled with the population explosion. As a result, housework ceased to be a full time occupation, and men's support for it as a full time occupation dropped, driving women out of the home and into the professions [25, 27].

Privacy itself can create a power differential. Some Middle Eastern women cover their bodies and keep their body shape and appearance private. Such cultural norms often have historical reasons that confer economic and political power. Body covering is universally practiced in the modern world, ranging from just the genitals in some parts of Africa and Southern European beaches, to all body in some parts of the Middle East. Middle Eastern women who cover their bodies basically created an implicit collusion not to compete with each other on the basis of appearance; and mate selection is done by families on the basis of other criteria. Such collusion supported by extended privacy is actually a source of power, similar to noncompetition agreements among corporations. It basically guarantees a mate to everyone irrespective of appearance, and it raises the price to be paid by men for a mate, in the form of emotional and financial commitments. Making sex and bodies private is the major tool to maintain this collusion. In some ancient societies where sex was commonly available to all with all, there was no interest in body covering, or sexual privacy.

All collusions also create incentives to defect. Those with a competitive advantage have an incentive to break the cartel, compete aggressively for mates by breaking the rules, and gain an advantage at the expense of others. Women collectively enforce the dress code in every society to limit sexual competition, but every individual has an incentive to compete aggressively within the rules, or by pushing the rules at the edges slightly to gain a competitive edge, but without attracting the wrath of other women and being called a "slut".

Sexual norms follow the same pattern. Monogamy limits competition among men for mates, and prevents most powerful men from dominating the market with multiple partners, and leaving most others without a mate. Chastity limits competition among women, which keeps sex restricted to socially sanctioned relationships, and keeps the price of sex high for men. But new technologies create threats to these collusive agreements, and provide opportunities to break the cartels, and benefit individually, at the expense of the group. These technologies vary from creative clothing and makeup to body modification technologies, from birth control and abortion to women's professionalization.

Clothing and make up technologies are used extensively in the modern world, to change one's appearance, and to gain a competitive edge in sexual competition. It is a technology driven competition since textiles, oil based chemicals, and various body modification techniques from ear and nose piercings to Botox injections and breast augmentation surgeries drive the competition. Women are usually most obsessed with clothing, makeup, and body modification in modern world, because they compete with each other on the basis of appearance. But that is by no means universal since one can find male obsession with appearance and cosmetics in some ancient societies. In the grand scheme of societies, the norms of competition are quite arbitrary, and depend on how the society is structured, what roles are assigned to whom, what alliances and collusions are in place, and what technologies are available to compete on what basis [33].

Circumcision is another example of body modification, but by men. It probably started as a cosmetic procedure to make the penis look erect even when it is placid, to make the male more desirable in mate selection. It is similar in function to an ancient African tribal tradition of wearing an erect penis mask on top of one's own penis, to make it look erect, and to stimulate women. Circumcision is also a power exercise, by powerful men over powerless boys. It usually involves a powerful tribal and religious leader, and it demands the submission of an important and sensitive body part to violent manipulation. In that sense, it is similar to hazing or bullying where the purpose is the exercise of power, both for the psychological pleasure of the powerful, but also to prime the new member and his family for obedience. Harassment of minorities, foreign born, gays, homeless, disabled, prostitutes and any other powerless groups serves the same purpose. They are not harassed because people hate them. They are harassed because they are weak and defenseless, and they provide an opportunity for the powerful to assert their dominance, and to build group cohesion among themselves by identifying the in-group and the outsiders. It is no coincidence that such harassment is often done by groups where there is strong group cohesion. Social Networks can exacerbate such group behavior, if they can assist in cohesive and exclusive group formation, as many bullying incidents on Facebook demonstrate [7].

CHAPTER 11
TRANSPARENCY

Privacy is a double edged sword. It allows freedom of behavior by hiding that behavior from powerful groups, but it also isolates that behavior and prevents its spread to a larger community of support. Consequently, social movements still take a long time to develop, and still require major sacrifices from their leaders. Consider modern terrorism and insurgent movements. Before the age of distributed communication technologies, like the internet and satellite phones, an insurgent movement had to declare its intentions publicly and challenge the national government, which quickly led to an armed conflict. This is what happened in Cuba in 1950's when Fidel Castro formed a resistance movement and publicly declared his communist manifesto. With modern communication technologies, terrorists and insurgents can remain under the radar and private for long periods of time, while disseminating information and gaining recruits and support. Osama Bin Laden's anti American and anti-Saudi movement was operating for years by distributing sermons over the internet chat rooms and on compact disks, before it was recognized as a major threat.

All social and political movements have to strike a delicate balance between privacy and transparency. This precarious balance can be improved in two different ways: Increasing privacy rights is often advocated to support the powerless against oppression, because then they could build social movements without an immediate violent confrontation, but by spreading ideas, and that may benefit all parties. But paradoxically, increasing transparency may also help social movements, by allowing them to spread ideas more freely and widely. The confusion arises because privacy and transparency are not universal and equally distributed. The results depend on who has privacy, and who is transparent, and who has access to whose information. Powerful groups, such as governments and large corporations, benefit from their own privacy, while observing others unimpeded. Increasing privacy of the masses can reduce the power differential, provided that it doesn't also increase the privacy of the powerful elites. Wide-spread availability of privacy enhancing technologies, such as encryption or anonymous publishing, benefit the powerless more, but uniform availability of technologies to all is not easy to achieve. Powerful groups also benefit from others' transparency, while they hide their own information. Wide spread availability of transparency inducing technologies like citizen journalism and internet publishing can benefit the powerless more, but it is difficult to have a uniform wide-spread availability of technologies.

If both enhanced privacy and enhanced transparency can achieve the same goal, as long as they are widely available, then an obvious question is which would be the better approach and for whom? Privacy gets all the attention, but increased transparency for all may have a number of serious advantages over increased privacy, and may even lead to win-win situations for all, rather than a zero-sum game between various groups.

First, enhanced transparency may be easier to achieve then enhanced privacy. New communication technologies encourage openness, and make it easy to track and monitor others. Social media is at the forefront of the push for openness, to the dismay of many privacy advocates. Despite increasingly louder calls to protect ourselves by limiting our exposure to social media, there is an increasing willingness by many to divulge the minute details of their lives and their thoughts to the general public. That tendency is understandable, because you cannot take advantage of the social media fully if you do not embrace transparency fully. Protecting your privacy often means isolating yourself from friends and potential friends, and hiding your activities and thoughts that might otherwise lead to making meaningful connections with others who have similar activities and thoughts.

Mobile phones and GPS devices go further and make our physical location and physical activities available to the public and commercial interests. Opting out of those services would also limit access to many social and commercial opportunities. Finally, networking of objects equipped with sensors and cameras are likely to amplify this push towards complete transparency. All objects reporting their status constantly would expand social networks to include object networks, and together they would constitute a universal tracking system. Consider a sensor network that detects pollution discharge into a lake, a GPS system that tracks all vehicles that carry industrial waste, and a social network that tracks all personnel that process industrial waste. Together, they can pinpoint and track all pollution from its source to its destination. Such systems can be sued to implement effective pollution control systems with appropriate fees, penalties, and taxes, computed automatically according to the public cost of all activities. Without such extensive transparency, it is difficult to manage public goods [31].

Second, increasing transparency may achieve the same goals as increasing privacy, by reducing the power differential in society, because powerful groups benefit disproportionately from their privacy by observing others unimpeded. Transparency cuts into that power base. That is why WikiLeaks has been such a threat to governments and large corporations all over the world. It not only promotes complete transparency, but it also utilizes and independent and unedited medium to collect insider information from whistle blowers, and deliver it to the public. Twitter and mobile phone networks have been credited with the transparency that led to the organization of large protests in Tunisia, Egypt, and Iran in 2011. AT&T and Verizon were sued by the ACLU in 2006 for cooperating with the US government in monitoring all international emails and calls of US citizens, which are transparent to their servers. Cell phone companies reported in 2012 that they had received a whopping 1.3 million requests from the government for phone records of US citizens in one year, overwhelming majority of which without a court order. Clearly, transparency is the order of the day, and privacy is difficult to achieve. It may be more effective to simply expand transparency to all, including the governments and the corporations [21, 29].

Third, transparency allows the spread of ideas faster, and may support social movements, but there is a need to protect opinion leaders from early retaliation. That can be accomplished by creating permanent community structures that precede the development of new movements, but designed to support them once developed. The ideas are generated and owned by the community as opposed to lone individuals, and that protects the individuals. Consider modern universities and think tanks. They are institutions designed to create new ideas and fuel social and technological revolutions. Yet their design precedes the generation of specific ideas, and the generated ideas belong to the institution. That protects the individuals against retaliation, and also provides a framework for publicity for and confidence in the new ideas. Such institutions can be duplicated for all social and political issues ranging from lifestyles and political movements, to business ventures and consumer decisions. Such communities of idea generation can be supported by the new technologies of social networks and group collaboration. In a way, this approach to social movements is similar to tribal societies, where the tribe precedes any political and social movement, and the members support whatever develops as the tribal position. Such a diffused power structure in tribal societies is the primary reason why tribal societies are difficult to dominate politically. They may also be an effective structure then to protect nascent social movements.

Fourth, social problems may be easier to solve with compete transparency. Many social issues have become similar to football games, where people take extreme positions, and engage in unending debates, for the purpose of winning just for winning's sake, rather trying to solve problems. Leaders benefit from these unending debates because they build careers out of debating. The followers benefit from them by building identities for themselves by identifying with one group or the other, often randomly, as they do with sports teams. They derive a psychological benefit of being important and belonging to a group, in an otherwise socially fragmented modern society. Issues like abortion, gun control, or gay marriage are rarely about what is debated, such as the science of when life begins, or the importance of second amendment, or social justice. They are about winning and losing. So, obvious compromise solutions are readily ignored by all involved. Transparency would make the real underlying issues and political interests visible, and the compromise solutions would be obvious. If abortion is really an economic struggle between professional women and homemakers, if gun control is really a political struggle between urban and rural populations, and gay marriage is really a power struggle between religious and secular elites, then solutions would be very different [25]. Fifth, transparency creates new social and economic opportunities. Social networks are already demonstrating some of these new opportunities, such as tracking friends' activities, and peer-to-peer recommendations. Financial applications such as peer-to-peer payments, peer-to-peer loans are likely to follow. But many other novel applications can emerge if consumers' needs and desires are transparent to each other, and they can form consumer communities around those needs and desires, such as transportation, food, home ownership or entertainment. Then, a community manager can execute transactions on behalf of all the members, and can represent their interests against business interests, leading to more expertise in consumer decision making, and more bargaining power. Consumption decisions are complex, and consumers are rarely well equipped to make those decisions individually. Even employment decisions can be delegated to such communities. All those with specific skills can join communities of career, and employers can contract with the appropriate community to fill positions. These communities would be different from job search firms that merely match employers with employees. Here, the contract would be between a business and a community, and the community would fill the position, take responsibility for the performance, and dynamically replace employees with others as necessary. In such an environment, economic discrimination against individuals by businesses is prevented, and the communities are less likely to discriminate arbitrarily, since they are self-managing organizations. Such communities are also in the best position to judge the qualifications of their members, and set up standards for continued membership in the community. Temp agencies operate like this, and legal and medical professions have professional communities and standards. Extending them to all professions and skills, and allowing them to make employment decisions, would require new organizational structures supported by an extensive technology infrastructure of transparency and information sharing [26, 30].

Sixth, transparency may lead to extensive resource sharing, and hence significant economic benefits for all. Although modern economies rely extensively on resource ownership and exclusive resource control by individuals, corporations, and governments, resource sharing has significant advantages by streamlining, optimizing, and even automating economic activities. Resource sharing has the potential to dramatically change the structure of economic and social institutions. As information technologies enable increasing transparency, they make it increasingly feasible to dynamically allocate resources, rather than to own them exclusively.

Consider car ownership versus car rentals or increasingly car sharing services. Exclusive ownership and exclusive use of a car requires little dynamic information and only a single long lasting transaction. The information and transparency requirements with rental cars and car sharing is much higher, since the cars need to be tracked; their availability has to be recorded and communicated; and an allocation system has to be developed to assign cars to customers. But once there is enough transparency in the system, sharing leads to a more efficient utilization of resources by reducing idle time, and allocating each component of the resource to the most productive use; but the information requirements, information processing costs, and threats to privacy are high. Hence, sharing becomes increasingly economically desirable as new information technologies, and technology induced systems and organizational architectures reduce the cost of information and encourage more transparency. Government services such as education, criminal justice, and defense are already results of complex arrangements of information and resource sharing between local, state, and federal governments. Religious communities sometimes share resources to provide integrated charity services, safe houses, soup kitchens, or lifestyle guidance. Families share resources to provide child care services as in babysitting cooperatives, emotional support as in extended families and neighborhood community centers, economic cooperation as in cooperative living arrangements. Businesses share resources in consortiums, standards bodies, research centers, and at corporate boards. Such shared services and cooperative arrangements can be extended greatly and made much more dynamic with the aid of new technologies and ever increasing transparency of resources. One can envision complex services created from components provided by multiple social institutions, or even superstructures imposed on the existing social institutions that allow individuals to enter and exit social arrangements dynamically on the basis of pre-specified goals. Super-governments such as the United Nations are already active in tackling intergovernmental problems such as environmental degradation, poverty, and epidemic diseases by sharing resources and information among member nations. Virtual Corporations composed of loosely coupled businesses already provide superstructures where businesses can band and disband quickly on the basis of pre-defined goals, and share resources. Social super structures where individuals can freely enter and exit individual institutions on the basis of predefined goals are yet to be designed. Examples are: individuals who can easily change their citizenship in response to national policies; localities that can change their affiliation by crossing state and national boundaries in support of various policies and political causes; individuals who can move between families and friendship networks connected through extended or super families as they change their residence; children raised by extended networks of families that are connected through virtual structures on the basis of specific values and child rearing philosophies; employees who can easily switch jobs between businesses that are linked by virtual super structures defined by common business goals, as their skills, needs, and family requirements change. These are all arguably feasible social arrangements, and may become increasingly more desirable as the new information technologies increase the transparency of information, facilitate sharing of resources, and track and reveal each individual's needs and requirements dynamically [26, 31].

Seventh, intellectual property can be protected in novel ways. Permanent communities can be built to support the creation of intellectual property. These communities can be modeled after universities where researchers are paid to create intellectual property, but once it is created it belongs to the public domain, and shared freely. Those who created valuable property are rewarded with continuing employment to create more, but the rewards are always for expected future creations, not for the past accomplishments per se. Payments to support such communities can be provided by governments, donations, foundations, but most importantly by value added services by the communities themselves such as support, education, consulting, live demos, lectures, performances, and social events, just like universities. One can easily imagine musician's communities that are supported by training new musicians, concerts, and live events, but the music created belongs to the public domain and shared by all freely. The members benefit from their reputation and continuing support for their creativity by the community, not by sales of products [26, 30].

All such initiatives require an extensive technology infrastructure to support extensive transparency of information, tracking and sharing of resources, and monitoring individuals' needs and performance, and more importantly to support extensive collaboration and cooperation by large organized communities.

PART 3
TECHNOLOGY AS RISK

Technology is not socially neutral, merely providing options.
What technology makes feasible, economics makes essential.

Technology is a source of risk. Not only because it often has unintended consequences, but also because accelerating technological change creates compound risks resulting from multiple interacting technologies. More importantly, a fast changing technological environment introduces additional risk because of the numerous social, economic, and political opportunities it creates, and threats it facilitates. In a competitive world, taking advantage of these new opportunities, and protecting against the emerging threats are constant battles both for individuals, and for businesses and governments. These risks are most pronounced in global communication, military, and banking systems, but no social institution is immune. Reduction of these risks should be a major concern for all social institutions, instead of merely dealing with undesirable consequences after they occur. There are numerous risk-reduction technologies that can be deployed to reduce risk while still maintaining the efficiencies created by efficiency-raising technologies.

CHAPTER 12
EFFICIENCY AND RISK

Technologies are created to change the world, by creating new efficiencies to meet immediate human needs. But such immediate efficiencies often introduce long-term uncertainty and risk, because the long-term consequences of new technologies are difficult to predict. There is a reason why most species on earth do not change their environment. Sharks, for example, have not changed in 100 million years according to the fossil record of shark teeth, although some very large shark species have gone extinct. Human ancestors on the other hand have been changing their environment and themselves constantly, and even only 100 thousand years ago, nothing closely resembling a modern human even existed. Compared to other species, humans are a risk taking species, a desperate species that is willing to take great risks to survive, probably because its survival was always precarious. Successful species do not take great risks with their already successful strategies. One theory suggests that human existence has always been precarious, and about 100 thousand years ago, human ancestors may have already faced imminent extinction, with their population going below a few thousand individuals. This is when Africa faced a great climate disaster, which presumably forced the survivors to migrate out of Africa in a desperate move to survive. Such risk-taking behavior continues unabated to this day [4, 20].

Consider agriculture. It created huge efficiencies in food production, by subjugating land, plants, and animals to serve human needs. But it also created huge risks in the long run, of deforestation, land erosion, environmental pollution, species extinction, and new plant, animal, and human diseases. Some of the most deadly epidemics in human history are probably the result of humans coming into close contact with domesticated animals, and consequently animal diseases mutating into human diseases, such as measles from pigs, small pox and tuberculosis from cows, influenza from chickens, and AIDS from monkeys. None of these consequences could have been predicted at the time of the adoption of animal domestication technologies, but the risk of such unexpected consequences is always present with any new technology [9].

Consider the automobile. It changed the efficiency of point to point individual transportation dramatically. Yet, it also introduced new risks due to urban air pollution and contribution to climate change. There is considerable evidence that despite efforts to control automobile exhaust, with modern emission control technologies and elimination of lead from fuel, urban air pollution may still be the cause of a great deal of illness, such as asthma. But the real issue is not what illness is caused by automobiles exactly, and how much of the climate change is due to automobile exhaust. Those heated debates are all taking place after the fact, and they are missing the point. The real issue with all technologies is that they introduce risk. The risk is difficult to estimate at the time of adoption, and it may be too late to alleviate the ill effects after the adoption. The critical issue is the risk of unknown future problems, not precise quantification of the known present problems. Yet, the latter gets all the attention from scientists, policy makers, and the public. For example, there are currently a number of disease epidemics in the US, such as diabetes, attention deficit disorder, depression, and autism, and their causes are not known; but the chemical pollution of the urban environment is a prime suspect in all of them. Add to them, all the future problems that we do not even foresee currently, and the risks are easier to contemplate and appreciate, without actually quantifying them [33].

The problem of risk is exacerbated by the fact that once the undesirable effects are realized, it may be difficult or even impossible to alleviate them. Consider the bow and arrow. That technology allowed hunting of fast running animals from a distance, and it made a huge difference in the efficiency of food production. Yet, it also made the warfare more distant and more deadly, and it created the possibility of an overwhelming and conclusive first strike, by a large number of bowmen from a distance, precluding the possibility of retaliation. Before this technology, such a first strike was impossible, since you had to approach the enemy, and pass through its sentries and lookouts. Of course, once the technology was invented, you could not avoid it, because it gave such an overwhelming short term advantage in food production and warfare, no matter how big the risk was to all involved in terms of the bloodiness of warfare and the danger of first strike in the long run. You had to acquire and deploy the technology. Later in technological evolution, nuclear weapons created the same risk of an overwhelming first strike from a distance, at the level of complete nations, which did not exist before. These new risks are impossible to quantify or even identify at the time of technology development [21].

Consider the automobile again. To accommodate increasing demand, expansion of the highway system has been relentless in the past 100 years. Yet, there is overwhelming evidence that building new highways create many unexpected risks, not the least of which is increasing traffic congestion! It is ironic that building highways to solve the traffic congestion problems actually makes it worse, by increasing the demand, through increased driving instead of relying on public transportation, more purchase of cars, and especially by building suburban housing along the new highways [14].

Propensity to take risk rises if you can pass the risk on to others, while you continue to benefit from the efficiencies. For example, airlines design their schedules to be very efficient to minimize fuel use and the idle time of personnel. So there is very little slack in the system. Yet, that increases the risk of a major disruption in operations whenever there is a failure anywhere in the system, since the failure propagates throughout the network when there is no slack in the system to absorb it. That's why a rain storm in Chicago can result in cancellation of flights from New York to Miami, by disrupting the flow of planes and personnel throughout the system. Airlines take too much of this type of risk, because the cost of disruption in the schedule is largely paid by the passengers, not the airline. Airlines simply cancel the flights and rebook the passengers on other flights. The loss of time and the experience of inconvenience by passengers do not fully factor into their design algorithms, because it is not their cost [3].

A similar issue arises in banking which leads to excessive risk taking and periodic financial crises. With every loan, there is a risk of default by the borrower. The banks tend to take too much of that risk, when they can pass it on to others, like government guarantees, securities created from the loans and sold to investors, insurance instruments that protect the banks from that risk, and government bailouts if the defaults threaten the banks' solvency. All of these opportunities to unload risk onto others creates incentives to take excessive risk, and leads to periodic crises when somebody else ends up paying for the excessive risk taken by a bank [17, 28].

The risk rises even more when communication and transportation technologies create connections that spread new technologies globally. In this highly connected environment, any new technology that provides a short term advantage is adopted universally, since when the markets are global, fierce competition punishes anyone who fails to adopt. Global markets are very efficient since they take advantage of resources and competitive advantages throughout the world; yet they also create new risks, because of homogeneity, since any failure will also be global. Consider the case of the lowly potato. It was discovered in America, and brought back to Europe. It had a number of advantages over other staple crops. It survived the harsh winters better; and it required less maintenance. So, the poorer peasant communities of Northern Europe increasingly relied on potato as the main staple. Then in 1845, the infamous potato beetle struck and devastated the potato crop for several years in a row. Since the population depended on potato for its survival to such a great extent, large scale famine followed in poorer peasant communities such as Ireland [7].

A more global risk exists in modern infectious disease epidemics. As human societies all adopt the same lifestyles because of global communication technologies, and get closely connected through transportation technologies, any disease epidemic spreads throughout the world within days. Any organism that finds a way to exploit a weakness in our lifestyle is likely to affect all humans and create a global crisis, as in global flu epidemics, when in the past such crises remained as isolated local problems.

CHAPTER 13
RATE OF CHANGE

Technologies introduce risk; constant change in technologies introduces constantly rising risk; accelerating technological change introduces accelerating rise in risk. As we celebrate our increasingly faster pace of technological change, we need to be cognizant of increasing risk for crises and catastrophes. It is the nature of the beast. Yet those risks are almost never seriously discussed when new technologies are being developed and considered for adoption, but delayed until the risks are realized and the problems start to emerge. By that time, it is often too late to block the unexpected consequences; so instead, the solutions often rely on developing even newer technologies to remedy the problems after the fact.

There are multiple complicating factors that lead to even higher risk for new technologies. First, the rapid introduction of new technologies can overwhelm the ability of humans and social institutions to absorb the changes and to adjust to them. An example is the cell phone. A variety of health risks have been conjectured in relation to the cell phone, ranging from exposure to radio waves, to neck and wrist injuries from constant use. But the biggest risk comes from our inability to adjust our lifestyles to the cell phone, but instead incorporating them directly into our existing activities such as driving and walking in traffic. Talking on the phone while driving, or even walking in traffic, has become a major source of accidents, which was not foreseen as a risk at the time of development and adoption of the technology. There are many other possible risks that are still not well understood, including the long term psychological and professional effects of being in constant contact with a small number of friends and colleagues. The effect of those intrusions into our privacy and our "alone" time are still just vague conjectures, even so many years after the introduction of the technology [10, 30]

Risk rises when many technologies are introduced in rapid succession and their social effects interact with each other, leading to compound effects. This risk is most pronounced in introducing new synthetic chemicals to the environment. Not only each new chemical introduces risk to the environment that is difficult to assess, but combinations of chemicals can have a qualitatively different impact than each alone. Our scientific understanding of such compound effects is minimal, and in fact the scientific method does not easily lend itself to such studies. Especially in statistical analysis, there is a tendency to focus on one variable at a time while holding others constant; but compound effects require a combinatorial analysis of looking at all possible combinations of variables, which gets unwieldy and impractical very quickly. There are numerous theories that suggest that some of the most intractable modern diseases such as obesity, diabetes, cancer, heart disease, allergies, depression, and autism may have multiple and compound causes, and that may be the reason for their intractability. There is new evidence for example that suggests that our modern sedentary lifestyle, as unhealthy as it is, may not be a factor in causing the obesity epidemic. It may be multiple factors in combination, such as what we eat, how much we eat, and some environmental pollutants called endocrine disrupters that disrupt our appetite regulation, and make us want to eat more than necessary in the first place. A consequence of this finding is that exercise may not help you lose weight [27].

A more complex example involves asthma, allergies, and autism; three modern epidemics that are poorly understood, and even more poorly treated. There is new evidence suggesting that all three may be auto-immune diseases and triggered by an infection of the mother during pregnancy. Strangely, it is not the infection that damages the fetus, but it is the immune reaction of the mother to the infection. The critical question is why then, the rates of these diseases have been skyrocketing to epidemic levels, when the infection rates of mothers have not changed or even declined in recent years. The answer turns out to be changes in mothers' bodies that are increasingly overreacting to infections, and producing disproportionately strong immune responses. The evidence suggests that the reason for such overreaction is our sterile, urban, and chemically and pharmaceutically saturated environment that isolates us from certain micro-organisms and parasites that are common in the natural environment of soil, water, and plants. Exposure to those micro-organisms and parasites turns out to be critical to build the human immune system and to regulate it. Lack of life time exposure to them leaves our immune systems underdeveloped, and any infection that is common in the congested urban environment causes an overreaction by such an immune system. Such a compound risk that involves lack of exposure to certain microorganisms, but extra exposure to other infection-causing organisms, is difficult to identify and even more difficult to remedy. The technologies creating these compound risks are also multiple, varied, and not simultaneously developed, as in urban development, transportation, housing, deforestation, agricultural, chemical and pharmaceutical technologies [33].

More importantly, vicious cycles and arms races may result from the introduction of new technologies, leading to a dramatic increase in risk. Technology companies are increasingly relying on constant change and innovation for competitive advantage, because many new technologies are information-based and are easy to imitate. Companies like Apple, Google, and Amazon are changing from year to year, with sometimes completely new products, and even new business models. In that kind of environment, there is very little time to adjust to the new technologies and adapt the social norms and institutions to them, raising the risk of repetitive and sequential compound effects. Consider cell phone. The major advantage of the cell phone was its portability, and hence using them in cars was the most popular early application. Soon after, texting came along, before the social norms could adjust to the voice calls from a car; and texting from a car immediately became the new norm. Now, texting while driving is a major threat to the lives of motorists, because it requires taking your eyes off the road and looking at a screen. If texting had been invented before voice calls on cell phones, one would suspect it would not have gained support as a car activity. Such sequence effects are very common when various versions of a technology are introduced in rapid succession, with no opportunity to adjust to each separately [29, 30].

An interesting example is fighter planes. This technology created a decisive advantage in a variety of wars from WW2 and Vietnam in 20th century to Iraq and Libyan wars in the 21st. Consequently, there is a never-ending race to improve their speed and maneuverability, ahead of our adversaries. But the increasing complexity and accuracy of air wars are creating unexpected risks. Starting with Second World War, air power consistently expanded the definition of battle field, first to include industrial sites that support the war effort, then to infrastructure like highways and bridges that may be used for military purposes, and eventually to all economic and civilian targets that support the war effort. However such increasing expansion of the battle field upends centuries of rules of war, eliminates the distinctions between civilian and military, and leads to the wholesale destruction of complete cities as in the bombing of Dresden and the nuclear destruction of Hiroshima in WW2, and the decimation of forests in Vietnam. Consequently, it increasingly eliminates the distinction between military operation and terrorism, by targeting civilians. The latest entry into this arena is unmanned drones. They increase the confusion further by targeting the enemy's civilian leadership, often in their homes, along with their families; and they are controlled from distant civilian areas, basically making the whole world a battle field. Arms races create unending and continuously compounding risks [23].

Finally, and probably the least intuitive risk from technological change is the political turmoil it creates. New technologies do not impact all equally. Technology is not like a gentle rain that falls on all equally, as Buddha suggested in the parable of the medicinal herbs. It is more like a thunderstorm that benefits some, but devastates others. Fast changing technological environment mobilizes all segments of the society politically, to gain economic advantages over others, by deploying the new technologies that serve their economic interests, and by preventing the deployment of technologies that threatens their interests. They accomplish this by encouraging and pushing the adoption of self-serving technologies, but discouraging or even legally banning threatening technologies. Such political activity is costly to the society, and may even lead to lose-lose situations despite costly efforts by all sides. The primary reason for such political risk of lose-lose outcomes is because adversarial systems do not always lead to optimum solutions. In an effort to create the maximum advantage for themselves, political groups often take extreme positions for negotiation, but then they are locked into those extreme positions when they declare them as moral principles, and find themselves in unending political struggles, unable to compromise on their moral positions. Even when one group wins the debate temporarily, they are rarely satisfied, because the extreme positions they took were not the optimum and stable outcome in the first place. That is why any victory stimulates even more extreme opposition from the losers of the debate, and changing technology disrupts any victory and creates new political struggles and opportunities in short order [6].

Consider birth control, and abortion technologies. They created wonderful opportunities to control the timing of parenthood, and to build professional careers unencumbered by parenthood responsibilities. But in the process, they disrupted the dominance of marriage as the defining institution of modern life, with one partner as a full time homemaker. They gave an advantage to professional women over homemakers, who could now delay child birth and focus on their careers. That advantage soon turned into an expectation, as men overwhelmingly preferred to marry women who could make a living in the job market, instead of relying on their husbands for support. That attack on homemaking as a job created a vicious political struggle with extreme positions taken on either side, when there are many easy and obvious compromises available. Even if abortion was completely outlawed, as some advocate, the proponents would probably still not be satisfied, as it would not be a very desirable society, and those who are terribly disadvantaged by that development would react forcefully and even violently. More importantly, as the birth control and abortion technologies change, the struggle is renewed with new parameters and arguments, new moral principles and new extreme positions, such as the beginning of life at conception and even earlier, first trimester survivability of the fetus out of the womb, morning after pill as abortion, exceptions for rape and incest, whether pregnancy is common in case of rape even though rape treatment in every hospital includes highly effective pregnancy prevention, and a myriad of other tangential issues which have nothing to do with the political struggle. As the positions become entrenched and increasingly couched in moral principles to rally the simple folk, the rank and file, the underlying political issues are forgotten, and a compromise becomes impossible. The social cost of such unending political debates and struggles is astronomical, especially if they turn violent [16].

Similar debates take place about environmental pollution. Industry often takes the extreme position of new chemicals being considered completely safe until there is conclusive evidence that they are harmful. Even with considerable evidence to the contrary, the debaters may get locked into their positions. Jack Welch, former CEO of General Electric, once claimed that PCB's were completely safe, and the pollution of the Hudson River was exaggerated, since as a young chemist, he was in PCB's "elbow deep" every day, with no harmful health effects [22]. Similarly, some environmentalists would like to ban all new synthetic chemicals until they are conclusively proven to be safe to all humans, animals, and plants. Such extreme positions do not lead to useful compromises; and with thousands of new chemicals being introduced to the environment every year, it is difficult to reach a reasonable conclusion to this debate. In a fast changing technological environment, with entrenched interests constantly threatened, it is difficult to have reasonable compromises and make reasonable policy decisions. Instead, unending debates create a class of professional debaters, building a career out of representing various interests. They tend to be ideologues and demagogues, with no serious interest in finding compromises, since their own interests are in building careers out of unending political struggles [10, 16].

CHAPTER 14
PREDICTION AND RISK

Statistical analysis provides the tools for studying risk and making predictions, and statistics has also become the mainstay of discovery and analysis in social sciences. There are numerous and fundamental problems with the extensive reliance on statistics to study and evaluate risk, and to predict and remedy its consequences. First and most obvious is that it takes attention away from the domain knowledge and insight, and places the emphasis on formal statistical tools. John Kenneth Galbraith, Harvard economist and past president of American Economic Association, once famously lamented that statistical analysis had impoverished economic studies, by focusing too much on quantification, at the expense of insight. Unfortunately, insight is critical to developing solutions to social and economic problems. Statistical analysis may find relationships among existing phenomena, but does not find solutions to change the undesirable phenomena. Solutions require insight into causality, not just relationship and correlation among variables. More importantly, without causal explanations and insight, statistical relationships are often interpreted as suggesting the most obvious solutions, when in fact proper solutions can be far from obvious. Such statistical studies of risk ironically carry a huge risk themselves of missing the causes, explanations, and the consequences of risk, leading to inappropriate responses. Judea Pearl, UCLA statistician, once argued humorously that in every academic paper there is one section that is completely nonscientific, and it is always titled "conclusions". Statistical analysis rarely gives you enough insight into causes of social issues to allow drawing correct policy conclusions [11, 26].

Consider the statistical finding that children who grow up with two parents are healthier and more successful in life. The immediate and obvious policy conclusion is to support the marriage institution and to discourage divorce. In fact, that might be the wrong policy conclusion without further insight. One needs to understand why people divorce and how that affects children, which is called the process or domain knowledge. For example, it is possible that if you separate good marriages and bad marriages, the children of bad marriages may be better off after a divorce. If you distinguish between amicable divorces and hostile divorces, the children of amicable divorces may be healthier and more successful than the children of married couples. And those are just two simple examples. There are infinitely many such variables that may allow fine tuning of any statistical analysis, such that without a detailed qualitative understanding of the divorce process and how it affects children, it would be difficult to draw a policy conclusion from a purely statistical analysis. Without such insight, calculating the risk to children from divorce would be too general to be useful, or even fundamentally incorrect [26].

Adding to the difficulty, statistical analysis focuses on expected risk, not the risk of extremes and catastrophes. Gamblers for example often calculate their odds of winning, but the expected value may not be very useful. Even if the expected value was positive, most gamblers end up losing against the house, because when the oscillations between wins and losses are large, most people quit when they run out of money. Of course, that is exactly the wrong time to quit, but a gambler with limited funds has no choice. A good example of this is the "sure win" strategy that is often espoused by roulette players. The idea is to simply double your bet after every loss, and start over after every win. If winning pays double, then your expected winnings are always positive, as long as you don't quit immediately after a loss, but double down as your strategy requires. Yet, most people lose anyway, because you need a large sum of money to be able to continue doubling your bet, and when you run out of money, you can't continue. So, the critical risk is the risk of a catastrophe, which is running out of funds, not the expected risk by playing indefinitely [32].

The gambling example has many real world analogs. Nassim Taleb argues in his book *The Black Swan* that this is a fundamental problem in financial markets where expected risk and return is commonly used to evaluate investments. But the rare financial crises may be the determining factor for most investors and businesses. Such rare events are rarely factored into risk/return calculations, because they are difficult to predict, and even impossible if they never happened before. Yet, they could be devastating to investors and businesses, since a single crisis can force them out of the market after a big loss, and at precisely the wrong time to quit. He gives the example of not predicting the possibility of a black swan, since in Europe all swans were white, until black swans were discovered in Australia. A black swan type of crisis, which has never been seen before, is impossible to predict. Yet, financial engineering technologies are constantly introducing new financial instruments that create new risks of catastrophe, which are impossible to predict, because they have never happened before since the technologies did not exist before [32].

More importantly, statistical analysis focuses on precision and correctness in a narrow domain, under strict assumptions, at the expense of intuitive concepts and general principles that are roughly correct but apply broadly. The precision and reliability of analytical models become liabilities if they lead to overconfidence and overgeneralization. Specificity and precision do not imply broad applicability. On the contrary, analytical models are often very brittle, and when their (not necessarily realistic) assumptions are not satisfied, they can fail dramatically. Moreover, the abstractions of the analytical models increase the opaqueness of their assumptions, and raise the danger of overgeneralizing. Broad qualitative insights on the other hand are often roughly correct and lack precision, but apply more generally and with fewer and more transparent assumptions. For example, during the 2008 financial crisis, former Federal Reserve chairman Alan Greenspan famously acknowledged that the financial markets had failed to obey some basic assumptions made in their analytical models, such as self-correcting, and accurately judging their own long term self-interest. Without those basic assumptions, most analytical models could not reliably predict market behavior, even in the aggregate. With constantly changing financial engineering technologies, the ability to predict the behavior of financial markets, and to judge the impact of specific Federal Reserve actions is even more suspect [17, 32].

Similarly, extreme and rare rewards are often ignored in statistical models, but in fact they might be the primary driver of human behavior. This might be the reason why people buy lottery tickets, although their chances of winning are very low, and the expected value of the ticket is always less than the cost. But money does not have linear utility. The value of a large win is so high that it dominates the decision process. This is the same reason why people commit property crimes, although they are likely to be caught and punished, and the expected value of the crime is less than the cost of punishment. But the value generated from crime can be so high in the rare case of not being caught, or in the brief period before being caught, that it dominates the decision process, especially because the cost of punishment comes later and gradually over a long period of jail time. Especially for those whose lives are not very rewarding and meaningful, the cost of punishment may be minimal, since a prison life may not be terribly different from a difficult life in a crowded and dangerous inner city slum. Even the death penalty may not be a deterrent for someone with a dismal life, if the reward can be a life changing experience, at least briefly. Crimes of passion, sex crimes, drug crimes, property crimes all have this quality; and punishment may not be an effective deterrent, as high rates of recidivism also confirm. Punishment for crime may be merely an opportunity to take revenge and to get psychological satisfaction. If the purpose of punishment is deterrence, the system of punishment has to be reassessed, as technologies of crime change the rewards and risks, but also the technologies of crime prevention such as monitoring and tracking become more effective. Deterrence requires an emphasis on prevention, not punishment after the fact [2, 18].

Finally, statistical analysis in social sciences often focuses on a typical or average subject, but very few people are actually typical or average, so the results may not apply perfectly to most people. Average marriage lasts seven years, but that may not be relevant to most people who do not have average marriages. The expected value does not tell us why and under what conditions the expected duration might change, and there may be infinitely many such conditions and factors in evaluating the risk in any particular marriage. More importantly, the expected value doesn't tell us the worst case scenarios, and under what conditions they might take place. Vague but intuitive insights into marriages and what makes them fail in general may be more useful than the expected duration, or even the variance, as they provide policy guidelines by inferring causality [1, 32]

CHAPTER 15
MONEY AND RISK

Money introduces risk to an economy, since it is an IOU issued by a central bank, and all IOU's carry the risk of change in value in terms of purchasing power, or even a complete loss of value when the IOU's are not honored. National currencies have the former risk because the central bank controls the amount of currency in circulation and hence its purchasing power; and private IOU's such as bank loans have the latter risk since the issuers may default and fail to honor the IOU. These risks are multiplied when banks loan to each other and the failure of one bank affects all the others. Central management of money by central banks and governments adds to this risk, since their decisions all other banks and the complete economy of the nation, and financial crises are difficult to localize. Finally, interbank relationships among the central banks of different nations, and among the private banks of different nations, make any crisis in any part of the world a global crisis. Such centralization and interconnection in the financial world is relatively new in history and unprecedented. It is yet another example modern communication technologies creating great global efficiencies, and along with it, huge global risks. This global financial system leads to repeated financial crises, because centralization leads to information overload, and makes decisions very complex; and global interconnection spreads the effect of any faulty decision globally. That combination of the difficulty of complex centralized decisions, and the global impact of any faulty decision creates an extremely risky environment [28, 34].

There are alternatives, and it hasn't always been this way. Ancient barter economies of the early agricultural societies, although much less efficient, did not have any of these risks. Local banking systems of early industrial societies, isolated from the international financial system, had their risks localized. Crises were common, but did not escalate into global crises. Even the risk of a national currency was often reduced by private currencies issued by private banks, local currencies issued by local governments, or barter economies that existed alongside the national currency. None of these schemes were very efficient, because of their inability to take advantage of global opportunities and exchanges, thereby leading to the development of more efficient, but more risky, global financial systems. But new information technologies are making many of these ancient techniques of risk reduction feasible again, and even more desirable, by reducing their inefficiencies, while still maintaining their low risk [15].

National money is debt created by national governments or by regulated commercial banks. It is managed centrally, with all the consequent problems of central management, such as information overload at the center, single point of failure, and incentives for political struggle to influence and corrupt the decision makers. A distributed and decentralized management of money would alleviate these problems. There is some historical precedence for decentralized management of money in the United States. In early 19th century, many commercial banks issued their own private currency, and the federal government largely stayed out of the money business. By mid 19th century, there were approximately 30,000 different private currencies in the United States. There were many problems with such decentralized management of money through private currencies, such as the non-universal acceptance of money, the risk of bank default, and the difficulty of consistent currency exchange among all the different currencies. Modern information technologies can be used to solve these problems while maintaining all the advantages of decentralized management. Communication networks can be used to connect all currency issuers for universal acceptance of all currencies; social networks and recommendation systems can be used to collectively judge the default risk of currency issuers; and electronic exchanges can be used to automatically exchange currencies to support multi-currency transactions [19, 34].

Imagine a new monetary environment where all businesses, and even some individuals, can issue private money as credit to their suppliers and employees. Such private money is merely an electronic IOU signed by a business in exchange for goods and services. It is fundamentally different from debt-based money, since it is issued only in exchange for goods and services, and hence its quantity is expected to be self-regulating. It is implemented merely as an electronic record in a database shared by all parties involved. The shared database can be housed and maintained by a third party electronic marketplace, or merely duplicated as a shared electronic record in the databases of all parties. Such shared inter-organizational databases have been studied in great detail, and they are used extensively in building electronic exchanges and auctions. They also have complex transparency requirements that reveal transactions and provide audit trails to all relevant parties, while hiding information from all others. In this environment, all businesses can act as currency exchangers by automatically accepting the currencies of their trusted business partners. A transaction between non-business partners is intermediated by others. Such intermediation can be completely automated, and go through many intermediaries before the two parties can be connected by a chain of intermediaries where each is trusted by the next. Each intermediary accepts the currency of a trusted partner, and replaces it with its own, before pushing the payment to another trusted partner, on its way to its ultimate destination. Such automated intermediation is similar to how internet operates as a distributed network, where a message goes through multiple intermediaries, called routers, before it reaches its destination. Such dynamic network management is well understood, where each node has extensive local information, but very limited global information [13, 15].

In this new monetary system, incentives are needed to encourage participation. Each intermediary can impose fees or commissions on each transaction it routes, for facilitating the movement of the payments through the network, and for guaranteeing the performance of their trusted partners by holding their currency. Each transaction, as it finds its way through the network, accumulates fees. The total would be charged to the originator of the transaction as a transaction fee. The computation of the best route to take through the network would involve an effort to minimize the total transaction fee. The problem is similar to the task of minimizing delay for each message in a computer network by considering the load and capacity at each node. Such routing algorithms are widely available, and they can be readily adapted to route selection for payments. Each business acts as a bank by accepting and exchanging the private currencies of its trusted partners, and thereby facilitating their transactions for a fee. In the process, each business may accumulate the currencies of its partners, if there is a deficit in trade balance. Excessive accumulation of a currency may prompt a business to stop accepting it, or to start charging a higher transaction fee for that currency. Basically, each business dynamically adjusts its transaction fees to earn more transaction income, while minimizing its exposure to default risk due to holding the currencies of its trusted partners. In other words, each business guarantees the credit worthiness of its trusted partners by holding their currency (in effect, extending a line of credit), and in return it benefits from the transaction fees paid by its trusted partners whenever they utilize its services as a currency exchange intermediary. Each business tries to find the optimum trade-off between the two by utilizing their knowledge of its business partners. The problem is similar to network design where each node benefits from the traffic flow it receives (i.e. transactions), and tries to maximize it within the limits of its capacity (i.e. risk tolerance). Each node of such a decentralized network has to decide which other nodes to connect to, and how much traffic to accept from each. Network design literature provides many algorithms to attack this general problem [12, 13].

Banking is dramatically altered in this new environment. The need for formal bank loans is minimized, since the distributed management of money enables extending credit automatically to one's business partners, and indirectly to others, by merely accepting their private currency. Each business utilizes its knowledge of its business partners to judge their credit-worthiness, and decides on the credit line to extend to them. In effect, formal bank loans are replaced by the network of business relationships, and the collective and distributed judgment of credit-worthiness within the network. This results in decentralization of control and management of the money supply. Default risk of a business is also distributed among all its partners that hold its currency. In effect, businesses use their knowledge of each other in performing these intermediary roles, and judging each other's credit worthiness. Such knowledge is acquired during the normal course of business, but needs to be supported by a legal framework that requires transparency. Businesses need to reveal the identities of their partners, and the amount of currency (credit) they have issued to each partner. Businesses need to be able to observe the underlying assets and the total currency issues (debt) of their partners to judge their credit-worthiness, to facilitate the distributed peer-to-peer payments without any central control. Such transparency can be implemented by independent electronic exchanges that keep public records of all transactions among partner businesses, and their outstanding currency balances. Industry-wide electronic exchanges are common, and the technologies to implement them are widely available in terms of industry standards, or inter-organizational data exchange [8, 12].

Credit risk is fundamentally different in this new environment. At the most detailed level, how much a business is willing to hold the currency of another is a measure of trust it places on the other's credit (trust). How much a business already holds the currency of another is a measure of relative financial strength (collateral). At the most aggregate level, how much of its own currency, all of its partners are willing to hold in total, is an indication of its credit-worthiness (credit). How much of its own currency, all of its partners already hold, is a measure of overall financial weakness (debt). The difference between the partners' total willingness to hold and the amount they actually hold (credit-debt) is a good measure of aggregate confidence in a business, leading to a realistic measure of future performance, since it is actually the difference between their aggregate credit and their aggregate debt. Conversely, a business that is holding a great deal of others' currency is a high performing business that does not have to issue large amounts of its own currency, and it is in a position of great power in deciding whose currency it will hold (i.e. extend a credit to) [12, 25].

There are many attempts to adopt such private currencies in the online world, leading to many profound experiments with money and banking. The translation of these ideas to the physical world is still some time away, due to numerous economic, technical, legal, and management challenges, but they are likely to fundamentally change the perception and reality of risk in the world of money and banking [8, 24, 31].

CHAPTER 16
RISK REDUCTION

Technology is a source of risk. Not only because it often has unintended consequences, but also because accelerating technological change creates compound risks resulting from multiple interacting technologies. More importantly, a fast changing technological environment introduces additional risk because of the numerous social, economic, and political opportunities it creates, and threats in engenders. Reduction of these risks should be a major concern for all social institutions, instead of merely dealing with undesirable consequences after they occur. There are numerous risk-reduction technologies that can be deployed to reduce risk without damaging the efficiencies created by other efficiency-creating technologies. Some of these risk reduction techniques are being deployed in virtual environments leading to interesting experiments and simulations. Translating these experiments to the physical world faces many challenges, since the physical world poses some unique problems. Nevertheless, the concept of risk, how we measure it, and how we treat it, are all likely to change dramatically as these risk reduction technologies are refined.

PART 4
TECHNOLOGY AND POLITICS

Technology is not like a gentle rain that falls equally on all, but it is more like a violent thunderstorm that nourishes some but devastates others.

Politics is the art of reconciling the individual self-interests of people into collective action. As such, it is a collaborative effort, and relies heavily on the technologies of communication and coordination. So much so, that politics is often characterized by the communication technologies of the era, as in newspaper, radio, television, or internet. Mass communication technologies such as radio and television revolutionized the methods of political organization, and drastically changed the required leadership qualities and the criteria for success. Before mass communication technologies, citizens relied on their personal contacts to find reliable information and to coordinate political action. Electronic social networks create an opportunity to return to an earlier model of information dissemination and political action, by disseminating information and coordinating action through personal networks, rather than public dissemination and mass appeal.

CHAPTER 17
TECHNOLOGY OF POLITICS

Politics is the art of reconciling the individual self-interests of people into collective action. As such, it is a collaborative effort, and relies heavily on the technologies of communication and coordination. So much so, that politics is often characterized by the communication technologies of the era, as in newspaper, radio, television, or internet. Similarly, international politics, often called diplomacy, is often characterized by the available technologies of warfare, as in nuclear bombs, aircraft carriers, warships, artillery, castles and moats, steel armor, cavalry, or stone spearhead, each of which radically transformed warfare and diplomacy during its time [4].

War is the primary means of introducing technology into politics. Technology dominates warfare; and warfare or the threat of warfare and violence dominates politics. Even domestic politics is largely shaped by threats of crime, civil unrest, rebellion, and civil war, which are enabled by the technologies of warfare. Civil disobedience which is often touted as an alternative to violence is rarely effective without the threat of actual violence. It is most effective when there is concurrent violence, and it can be offered as a compromise alternative to it. Even completely peaceful protests that are popular with students and labor are, at the core, threats of violence. That is why protests often involve economic damage to powerful interests, while risking injury and incarceration by protesters, to demonstrate the ability and willingness of the protesters to resort to violence if necessary. A protest is a communication tool to show how strongly the demonstrators feel about an issue, and how much they are willing to sacrifice to that end, without actually engaging in full scale violence. In that respect they are similar to animal fights over access to food and sex, by engaging in controlled and limited violence. Protests are theater; and the audience is both the potential allies to observe your dedication to the cause, and join in; and also the adversaries to see your willingness to fight and make sacrifices, and back off [26].

In ancient tribal warfare in Africa, it was common practice for the warring parties to line up against each other and exchange insults, and get into shouting matches, which served the same purpose as the modern nonviolent protests. If the insults and the shouting matches did not resolve the conflict by demonstrating power, resolve, and willingness to sacrifice, then the next step involved individuals from each side stepping forward for one-on-one fighting. This limited violence pitted the best fighters from each side against each other, in an effort to show strength and dedication, to resolve the conflict without full scale warfare. If none of these efforts communicated sufficient information about each side's strength and determination to facilitate and effective compromise, only then full scale warfare ensued with great losses on both sides [21].

Indian independence movement of the early 20th century is often given as a classic example of a non-violent political struggle. Mohandas Karamchand Gandhi is often claimed to be the architect of nonviolent resistance as a successful strategy against a much stronger and more technologically advanced adversary, in this case the British Empire. But it is often ignored that there were many violent resistance movements in early 20th century India, concurrent with the nonviolent movement, some supported by the International adversaries of the British, such as the Russians, and some advocating a violent overthrow of the whole British Colonial System, such as Bal Gangadhar Tilak. When the British finally accepted defeat, they conveniently credited the nonviolent movement, and discredited the violent resistance. It is often in everybody's interest, when the conflict ends, to reach a negotiated settlement along the lines advocated by the moderates and nonviolent resisters, and to allow them to take credit, for the sake of a final compromise settlement. When in fact, the more extremist and violent movements may have contributed to the struggle equally, if not more, by pressuring the other side to compromise, and push them towards the middle [1].

Similar arguments apply to the Civil Rights Movement of 1960s in the US. The movement glorifies Martin Luther King and his nonviolent movement, but largely ignores the Black

Panthers movement during the same period which was organizing riots and sometimes burning large sections of big cities like Los Angeles and Chicago. Their contribution is minimized by historians of the era, although it is doubtful that the nonviolent movement could have succeeded without the violent backdrop, threatening to disrupt the social and economic life of the country, and making the nonviolent approach appear the more acceptable, moderate, and compromising solution. Another example is the Irish Independence Movement where the political arm and the military arm of the Irish Republican Army appear to be at odds in terms of tactics, but in fact, one cannot succeed without the other. Yet another example is the Palestinian Independence struggle against Israel where Palestinian Liberation Organization advocating political settlement and Hamas advocating military resistance appear to be fighting against each other more than the common enemy, but one movement cannot succeed without the other. Every resistance movement needs both a violent military component, and a reconciliatory political movement, to put forward both the threat and the compromise [26].

The rise of the nonviolent approach itself is the result of modern mass communication and coordination technologies that allowed large masses to coordinate boycotts and protests, to inflict enough economic damage to be taken seriously, and to demonstrate and widely communicate an effective threat of violence, to gain negotiating power.

Changing technology always changes the nature of warfare, and the nature of political organization, because immense political power is gained from the use and control of weapons technologies. In low-tech tribal societies, the power tended to be diffuse within the tribe, as it was difficult to concentrate power. Those with special skills such as strength and agility to master the handheld weaponry such as spears and clubs tended to gain power. As educational technologies such writing, reading, and singing spread, the special skills also spread widely, and became less important as distinguishing factors, but instead ownership of superior technology started to dominate. Feudal societies relied on technologies of construction, such as building of castles, fortresses, bridges, and moats. The lords who presided over these structures were not characterized by their personal skills, but their ownership and control of these technologies, which were largely inherited or acquired thorough personal relationships. As the power of destructive technologies such gunpowder surpassed the ability of construction technologies, feudal structures crumbled. Empires and colonial powers are the direct consequences of transportation technologies, such as roadways, ships, domesticated horses and camels, which allowed projection of power over large distances. Logistics, the ability to manage the transportation system, and move goods, weapons, and soldiers is the defining characteristic of empires. However, as the weapons system spread widely to all continents, utilizing the very same transportation systems, local populations gained increasing power over the foreign forces arriving from distant lands to an unfamiliar and alien territory, and empires started to crumble. Colonialism and international corporatism, relying on local elites for the exploitation of resources in distant lands, emerged with the rise of long distance communication technologies, that allowed building long-distance alliances, and control them from a distance. Finally, with the spread of communication technologies to the masses, colonialism and corporatism are also ending throughout the world. The new democracy movements in the Middle East and in South America are enabled by large scale organization of the masses, against foreign supported elites, whether they are in government or in business, using new communication technologies ranging from cable television and cell phones to the internet and social networks [4].

The nature of warfare is a direct result of available technologies. One constant change in human warfare has been the gradual but ever-persistent move away from face-to-face and intimate fighting, in preference for distance fighting from increasingly larger distances. This trend starts early in human history with the invention of stone spear heads, which gave a huge competitive advantage to fighters, by keeping them out of reach of their opponents during a fight. The archeological evidence is strong that this technology spread through the human population very fast. It is also highly likely that this technology increased the brutality of warfare. If the enemy did not have the technology, then the distance advantage allows one group to devastate the enemy with no danger to their own group, and the distance dehumanizes the enemy and provides the psychological barrier to commit massacres. If the enemy also possesses the technology, the conflict is less likely, but still more brutal when it happens, because there is a need to strike a decisive first blow or suffer devastating losses. These arguments have not changed over millennia, and the development of nuclear weapons and distant delivery systems such as ballistic missiles led to the same fears and strategies. This persistent trend of fighting from an increasing distance continues to this day with ballistic missiles, aerial bombing, and drone warfare, where the fighting is done from huge distances, and the enemy is no more than a few dots on a computer screen [8].

One consequence of fighting distantly is the difficulty of separating fighters from non-combatants. In hand-to-hand combat, the combatants are local and clearly identifiable, and there is even an audience to watch and evaluate the fairness of the fight. Such combat is as much a spectator sport as it is a mortal struggle. In tribal warfare, it is not unusual for the parties to insult each other, to brag about their physical and sexual prowess and denigrate the other side's, wear masks and make up to emphasize their strength and determination and to intimidate the enemy, integrate the losing side into their tribe as lower class members or slaves or kill them in rituals that have meaning for the living, incorporate their women and children into their communities by raping them, owning them, or marrying them. All of these practices make war a very personal endeavor. Modern warfare on the other hand is very impersonal where the enemy is rarely seen or interacted with. As such, the distinction between the soldiers and the civilians that support them is increasingly difficult. This is where the traditional rules of warfare start to fail. During World War 2, aerial carpet bombing of major cities was a common practice. Consequently for the first time, the distinction between military sites and the civilian infrastructure that support them disappeared completely; and along with it, large civilian casualties became a necessary part of warfare, called "collateral damage". With nuclear explosions, this trend was extended beyond infrastructure to a complete civilian population, since the annihilation of a complete city is a blunt instrument that draws no distinction between various targets. This erosion of the boundaries of a battle field, along with the development of powerful yet compact explosives led to the modern "terrorist" movements. They are not a drastic deviation from conventional warfare anymore, but a natural consequence of the constant erosion of the boundaries between military and civilian in distant fighting. As a result, it is increasingly difficult to define a consistent set of rules of war. How is using drones to target political leaders of an insurgency different from an assassin shooting a political leader in a political rally? How is aerial bombing of a steel factory that is critical to the military campaign different from placing a bomb at a bank that financially supports the military operation? Yet, we are constantly asked to find subtle differences between them. In a way, modern warfare technology made us all terrorists, by impersonalizing war, by virtualizing it, and by blurring the boundaries between military and civilian [5].

The modern nation-state dominating the political landscape is also an artificial, impersonal, and mythical construct created by modern technologies. It is a formidable institution that imposes homogeneity on a population in language, culture, lifestyle, and religion, where one does not exist naturally. It imposes its will on its citizens, often violently. It demands sacrifice from its citizens in the form of taxes, military service, and obedience to laws made by those who control the state, and at the risk of losing liberty and life. It accomplishes all of these feats through extensive use of education, print and media technologies to indoctrinate the population into homogeneity; and by utilizing law enforcement, tracking and monitoring technologies to enforce compliance. But its primary advantage over earlier forms of political organization is its formidable capacity to mobilize resources, both financial and human, to wage war, and that is the main reason for its dominance in modern life [14].

Modern political theories are also driven by existing technologies, instead of being universal and fundamental. Slavery and slave-based economies are a direct result of large scale construction and agricultural technologies. Prior to development of those technologies, hunter-gatherer and subsistence farming societies had no use for slaves, since acquiring and controlling slaves was more costly than their potential contribution to hunting or small family farming. Centralization of power after the introduction of large scale agriculture led to an advantage from slave labor in the large construction, irrigation, religious, and defense projects throughout the world from European feudal lords to the Egyptian pharaohs. Empires fueled slavery further, because the need to fight large scale wars, and also to support large scale trading over long distances. American slavery was useful to the extent that there was a huge international market, and shipping technologies to access them, for the large amounts of sugar and cotton produced in Southern and Caribbean plantations. Industrialization of processing increased the demand for those raw materials from as far as the textile factories of England, and the sugar mills of Cuba to feed the large international markets [12].

As empires fell with the wide-spread distribution of weapons and manufacturing technologies, small scale artisan manufacturing and family farming gained economic power, since now they did not have to compete with kings, lords, fiefs, and aristocratic large land owners. That led to free market theories of capitalism. This political theory is based on an economy where each participant is small, yet well informed, and able to make rational decisions about distant markets to further his own interests. Such a model requires small scale artisan manufacturing and family farming technologies, and a print based information distribution system about markets and prices. Such a world existed only for a small period in time in human history! With large scale industrialization, capital intensive energy sources like oil, steam, and electricity, and the consequent economies of scale from large centralized manufacturing, that model quickly collapsed, and the economists started emphasizing market failures rather than market miracles. No modern business likes to operate in a free market that economists glorify, with a head-to-head price competition with a large number of competitors; and they will avoid it if they have the opportunity to. Businesses like to grow and control their markets, by acquiring their competitors or by simply driving them out of business, so that they can control prices, exploit their suppliers and their employees, and lock in their customers [22].

Marxist and socialist theories emerged in such an industrialized environment where a few large businesses controlled the market in every industry and every geographical location, and exploited their workers who were either too specialized to move to another industry, or to immobile to move to another location, or both. Government emerging as a counterforce to such powerful business interests is a direct result of heavy industrialization and large scale manufacturing and distribution technologies. The political conflict between government and business continues unabated to this day, because of the development of information and digital economies. Within the new information economies, the size and power of successful businesses continue to grow, since the ability to manage multi-national supply chains increases, and cross-border financial arrangements and international capital flow dominate progressively larger markets [22].

Information technologies created a new framework for the nation-state where myth creation and information control reached new heights. In nation states, leaders create myths, and the citizens identify with those myths and follow the leaders. In an information economy where the information is decoupled from individuals, and has an abstract existence, it is possible to create mythological leaders. The myth may involve a real person, but the image created may have little resemblance to the real person. Similarly, one can characterize and redefine one's political adversaries, and recreate their images into grossly distorted caricatures [23].

One can see examples of this in modern mythical leaders like Mao of China, Stalin of Russia, Lincoln of the US, Gandhi of

India, Ataturk of Turkey, Saddam of Iraq, Hitler of Germany where the idolized or cursed character, worshipped or despised by millions, had little resemblance to the real person. Elections in the US provide some of the best examples of image distortion. In 2004 elections, then senator John Kerry, a Vietnam war-hero with numerous commendations and medals, was transformed by his opponents into a traitor to his country, a war resister, by using some of his military colleagues to diminish his accomplishments and to distort his record. In 2008 elections, then senator Barack Obama was characterized as foreign born, Moslem, and socialist, in a massive effort of myth creation; when in fact he was Hawaii born, a practicing Christian, and a moderate centrist politician. In 1976 elections, then president Gerald Ford, an accomplished athlete throughout his life with varsity letters from University of Michigan, was portrayed as a stumbling uncoordinated klutz, and the image largely stuck and stayed with him for the rest of his life. [13]

It is a common tactic in US elections to characterize anybody who proposes a tax increase as a socialist, anybody who opposes abortions as anti-women, and anybody who espouses a religious point of view as anti-science. Such extreme characterizations are possible only through extensive use of technologies to edit, cut, paste, and distort images, videos, speeches, and text. Multimedia storage and distribution technologies make available, any comment made by any politician at any time in their lives, for searching, editing, rebroadcasting, and disseminating it to a large audience, isolated from its original context, and often deliberately edited to mislead.

CHAPTER 18
POLITICS OF TECHNOLOGY

Technologies do not have pre-ordained trajectories. They are created and developed in a social and political context, and that context pays a critical role in their trajectory of development and change. More importantly, the social and political context plays an even more important role after the development of a new technology, when its impact is clearer, by restricting or encouraging the use of the technology, through legal, economic, and social pressures [16].

A good example is abortion technologies. Modern abortion technologies were developed in 1960's with invention of flexible plastic suction tubes that did not damage the uterus. Of course, abortions were performed for millennia using a variety of traditional methods such as potions, poisons, application of heat or pressure to the abdomen, or inserting long and sharp objects into the vagina. Abortion was common especially after war related rapes, since raping women by invading forces was a common ancient war practice, as it was killing of the men. These were dangerous procedures, and they were not attempted lightly, since mortality rate was high due to perforations of uterus, bleeding, infections, and overdose from poisons. Yet, these dangerous procedures were not politicized, since they were not wide spread and used only in desperation. In ordinary circumstances children and pregnancy were highly prized and valued, and there were always many sexual prohibitions limiting sexual activity to procreation, which obviated the need for abortions. Politicization of abortion followed the professionalization of women after World War 2, and an emerging need to control and delay reproduction by professional women. Politicization is a direct result of the discomfort with professionalization of women, and the advantages that conferred to professional women over traditional homemakers. Those advantages were formidable, and changed the dynamic of competition among women for mates, changing the emphasis from beauty, personality, and housekeeping skills, to professional talent and employment. Consequently, it inflicted a major blow to the traditional family arrangement, and caused significant economic loss to those who benefited from that arrangement, like homemakers, and others who made a significant commitment to that lifestyle like men married to homemakers [19].

Weapons of modern warfare are also highly politicized. Some weapons and battlefield tactics are illegal under international laws and agreements, and there are increasing efforts to enforce those laws and agreements through international courts and war tribunals. There were always, implicit or explicit, rules of war, such as the treatment of women, children, and elderly, or the treatment of prisoners and surrendering soldiers, or the definitions of fair fight and just war. But the rules vary drastically over geography and time! Where do the rules come from, if they are not universal? Why is raping women by the invading forces perfectly accepted as the reward for winning the war in some cultures, yet it is an abominable war crime in others? Why are biological and chemical weapons such as Sarin gas and smallpox virus illegal, but other weapons such as napalm, cluster bombs, defoliating chemical agents, uranium tipped artillery, and land mines are perfectly legal? Such international protocols are rarely based on any moral principles, but they reflect the political power of various actors. Most often, they reflect the interests of nation-states over non-state actors; and at times they reflect the interest of powerful states against the weaker ones. Non-proliferation treaties are clearly designed to prevent more states from acquiring powerful weapons, such as nuclear, and lock in the monopoly of those who already have it. Anti-biological and chemical weapons treaties are designed to prevent non-state actors, such as insurgencies and independence movements, from gaining disproportionate power. Such laws are similar in many respects to the 19th century laws in the US that made it illegal for African-Americans to own guns; or European laws of the same period that prohibited their colonies from building or importing certain weapons systems such as warships and artillery [15].

Definition of war crimes follows a similar logic. Those activities that threaten powerful groups are often declared to be war crimes. High tech weaponry are the weapons of the powerful; and they are often considered to be more morally acceptable, despite their deadliness. Low tech weaponry on the other hand are often considered barbaric and immoral, even when they are as primitive as machetes, improvised explosives, and even rocks. Even nuclear weapons, which kill more indiscriminately than any other weapon system, are frequently justified as moral, because they "prevent" wars, or "shorten" wars by decisively terminating them. They become immoral only when they become widely available, and create a risk for the powerful players. Improvised explosives and missiles that are difficult to aim accurately are labeled terrorist weapons, because they can't be aimed exclusively to military targets, but nobody volunteers to supply those who use them with more accurately targetable weapons to prevent civilian casualties! Moreover, perfectly targetable weapons like cruise missiles and drone delivered hellfire missiles, when they miss their targets and kill civilians, are often excused as targeting errors, and the destruction is accepted as collateral damage. In fact, striking civilian targets causes mostly psychological damage, and does not significantly affect the outcome of a war, unless it is done in a massive scale. Similarly, when powerful nations assassinate political leaders or spokesmen for insurgencies, that is often labeled "self-defense" against terrorism; but if insurgent groups tried to assassinate political leaders or prominent journalists of major powers, that would unquestionably be labeled terrorism and declared illegal under international law [15].

Besides warfare, technologies of industrialization and information also created some of the most intense political struggles of the last century. Industrialization created huge business and public organizations, with highly specialized labor, to take advantage of economies of scale in industrial technologies, and the efficiency of specialization from coordination technologies. Coordination at such large scale, along with specialization at such small units, required a managerial class with special skills of coordination and communication, which never existed before outside of military. Information technologies further increased the reach and effectiveness of the managerial class, and concentrated power in their hands, creating a significant challenge to the power of capital owners. The ensuing power struggle between the ownership class and the managerial class is reminiscent of earlier power struggles between church and state, capital owners and clergy, and capital and labor; yet this latest power struggle is very poorly understood [11].

At the beginning of the industrial revolution, managerial and professional classes were merely agents of the owners, against labor; as with the case earlier in history with church being the agent of the ownership class. Karl Marx famously quipped in 19th century that religion was the "opium of the masses", presumably in favor of the aristocratic land owners. With the proliferation of information technologies and industrial automation, and increasing proportion of labor became intellectual labor, and joined the professional and managerial classes. Moreover, modern information technologies extended the reach of managers to all corners of the organization, and allowed them to centralize and control information and decision making, and create large organizational bureaucracies in the process, pursuing their own interests, instead of acting as mere agents of the owners and shareholders. There is some correspondence between the American intellectual Andrew Dickson and Karl Marx, with Dickson criticizing Marx's classic book Das Kapital for ignoring intellectual labor as a separate interest group, but treating them as agents of the ownership class. With the development of information technologies, Karl Marx's analysis may very well be obsolete, and replaced by a three-way power struggle among capital, labor, and professional class. There are many indications of such a trichotomy. Some examples of conflict between capital and professional class are the debates between corporate shareholders and managers over executive pay and corporate governance, and the debates between intellectuals, especially academe, and the capital owners, over the role and the size of government and taxes. Similarly, the conflict between professional classes and labor often presents itself as debates on social issues, such as the role of science versus religion in education and public life, urban versus rural issues such as gun control, sex and gender related lifestyle issues, and the differing emphasis on military expenditures and crime prevention. These issues arise because the two classes differ significantly in education and mobility, where they live and how they work, and the threats they face and the opportunities they see in new lifestyles [11].

Professional and managerial classes are rewarded on the basis of performance, and they justify their financial rewards as a return on their talents and their merit-based competitiveness. But raw talent is a genetically acquired trait, and in that respect, it is not terribly different from inheritance or royalty. The professional classes often criticize harshly the privileges of the aristocracy, royalty, and inherited wealth as unearned but merely inherited as birthright, yet they are perfectly comfortable with the privileges of talent and ability which are also unearned but inherited.

New technologies can make some talents relevant and advantageous, and turn other talents irrelevant and even burdensome. Those who were born with the right talents at the right time gain major advantages in life, and the relevant talents change with new technologies. Consider the technologies of subsistence hunting with spears and bows and arrows. They made the talents for running, throwing, and eye-hand coordination critically important; when in a gathering society those talents were rather irrelevant to survival. Later in agricultural societies, those talents lost their importance once again. With the recent emergence of information technologies, a number of previously unappreciated and even deprecated talents became critical to success, such as computer skills, attention to detail, and mathematical skills as opposed to social and communication skills, and this era has come to be known as the "age of nerds".

More importantly, professional and managerial classes emphasize the importance of certain talents and deemphasize others, to reinforce their power and to limit entry into their ranks.

This is why the entry into major professional fields such as medicine, law, and management is so difficult. The claim is that these fields are very intellectually demanding, and only the most talented few are qualified; but in fact those qualifications are determined by those who are already in the field, and they have an incentive to exaggerate the talent required to perform adequately. That self-serving exaggeration reinforces the importance of those fields, gives a psychological uplift to those already in the field, provides moral justification for their outsized financial rewards, and most importantly, limits entry into those fields, allowing the maintenance of those outsized rewards. The talent required to perform adequately in professional fields may not be nearly as stringent and rare as the proponents suggest in their self-serving claims [6].

Consider medical doctors. Admission criteria to medical schools are among the most stringent, admitting only 9% of all applicants, where roughly all fall into the top 1% of all college graduates. It would be difficult to justify why only the top 1% of all American college graduates are qualified to study medicine. Similar arguments apply to other professional fields. Equally important are the state and national certification exams which are equally demanding, and often used to block the graduates of foreign schools from practicing in the US. Finally, professional associations such as the American Medical Association AMA work diligently and lobby the US government to restrict immigration of professional from other countries, to keep the supply limited. Most of these efforts have little to do with enforcing quality, but a lot to do with reducing supply by restricting entry into the field to keep the professional incomes high. Online education with massive and open courses MOOCs threatens this model by potentially separating education from certification, and making education available to all freely through online resources. Then the only remaining gatekeeping function will be the certification exams, and since an exam is much easier to deliver than a complete professional education, they may be increasingly difficult to restrict, as many commercial and public organizations may move into certification business [10].

An unintended consequence of stringent admission requirements is the lack of diversity in some lucrative professional fields. There is a tendency for some racial and ethnic group to dominate a lucrative field, if they have some slight genetic or cultural advantage in that field on average. If the admission criteria are overly stringent and exaggerate the importance of such slight advantages, then you end up with a less culturally diverse profession unnecessarily.

Technologies impact different population segments differently, and that impact determines whether they will support the technology adoption or resist it, or even fight to ban its use to deny an advantage to their competitors and adversaries. Consider guns. Political analysts are perpetually surprised why the rural population in America stubbornly clings to an absolute right to own firearms with no restrictions, despite numerous massacres and tragedies involving high caliber semi-automatic weapons. They are extremely deadly at very high speeds, with no specific use except to kill people. Various theories have been advanced like nostalgia for an earlier rural America, paranoia about crime, distrust of government, or slippery slope worries. But none of them explain the extreme unwillingness to compromise. In fact the real reason might be the differential impact of the gun technology on rural and urban populations. Guns give an advantage to the rural population over their urban and suburban competitors, so not surprisingly, the support for uncompromising gun rights come predominantly from rural populations.

The advantage is not just the fact that guns are useful for hunting in rural areas, although they certainly are. The real advantage is the fact that guns are deadly to urban populations. Congested urban living, with high mobility and anonymity, high income disparity, and high incidences of mental problems due to lack of extended family and community structures, make guns intolerably deadly for urban populations. And that is precisely why rural populations support an uncompromising right to carry arms. Remember that there is no love lost between urban and rural populations, after a century of devastation of the rural social and economic landscape, in the hands of big corporate agriculture, big banks, and government agencies, all controlled by urban professionals. Conversely, it is no secret that urban professionals largely consider the rural lifestyle obsolete and quaint with more than a little contempt, and feel perfectly justified in fully exploiting their economic advantages over them. As the rural population bitterly complained about the exploitation they suffered for a hundred years, they were advised that new technologies create new realities and they need to accept their economic losses as a natural result of technological progress, and not view it as exploitation by a highly educated and organized urban cabal. But guns create the opposite economic reality from mechanized agriculture: they are not capital intensive; they do not require economies of scale; and they benefit the rural population at great expense to the urban and suburban. Let's be clear then: gun rights are popular with the rural population, not despite the massacres and tragedies guns cause; but precisely because of the massacres and tragedies they cause, since those tragedies are disproportionately impacting urban and suburban communities.

To political scientists, urban versus rural conflict is a very fundamental and a very common political struggle both in the US and around the world. Many social issues dominating the American political life are really urban-rural conflicts in disguise, precisely because the social impact of so many technologies is different on those two populations. Abortion technologies for example impact the populations differently, and give a big advantage to professional urban women, over the homemaking, child-rearing, and farm tending rural women. Consequently, as you would expect, the opposition to abortion is most pronounced in rural populations. Similarly, public universal education technologies benefit urban population with professional opportunities, but do little for the rural and agricultural segments of the country. Consequently, it is no surprise then that rural populations overwhelmingly side with the church, whenever there is a conflict between the secular public education and religious education, even when that religious education is shown to spread factual errors. Factual errors do not mean much when scientific education appears to be benefitting largely your adversaries, at your expense! This is a common conflict throughout the world, where the rural population finds religion as their only ally in their economic struggle against urban professionals, since it is the only institution that can challenge secular education that primarily benefits the urban population with professional opportunities.

Of course, no politician on either side of this conflict has an incentive to make this analysis explicit, and end up losing the support of the other side wholesale. Instead, they try to present the interests of their constituents as the "common good" for all, by relying on vague moral principles, rather than specific self-interest arguments. Democracy is a system where the winners are the ones who can convince you to vote against your self-interest because of a moral principle, while they vote for their self-interest!

In general, ownership and control of critical technologies confers benefits and leads to political struggle. Enforcing professional standards is only one method to restrict ownership and control. Owning critical resources is another. Private ownership of early railroads in the US in late 1800's led to considerable concentration of economic power, by enabling railroads to pick winners in transportation dependent industries. John D. Rockefeller, an oil industry tycoon at the time, took advantage of this power of the railroad companies to destroy his competition. He accomplished this by getting into secret deals with the railroad companies, for preferential treatment to his transportation dependent business, while raising the prices for his competition, which crushed them with exorbitant transportation costs. Once the competition is destroyed, the monopolistic alliance of railroads and oil companies raised the prices and enjoyed very high profits, until the government stepped in with the Interstate Commerce Act of 1887, and prohibited such secret deals, kickbacks, and predatory differential pricing [22].

A similar political struggle is taking place in the 21st century for the ownership and control of the internet. Internet was developed by the US government in 1970's, but later privatized with the condition of equal and open access by all, called "net neutrality", where equality refers to lack of discrimination with respect to content, and openness refers to lack of discrimination with respect to the devices connected. The telecommunications companies like Verizon and AT&T that now own the internet would like to change those conditions, and be able to restrict access and charge different prices to different users depending on the quality and speed requirements. Telecommunications companies argue that they can provide better service at the high end, such as guaranteed response time, if they can charge a premium price for it. In fact the struggle is a political one over who owns a critical resource and how much control they can exercise over it. The fear is that the owners of the internet may have the power to pick winners in network dependent industries, such as news and entertainment, as railroads did about 150 years before. Although laws now prevent such secret deals and predatory pricing, discrimination on the basis of arcane technical characteristics of the content or the connected devices may be used in subtle ways to provide preferential treatment to preferred businesses. The ultimate solution may come in building multiple competitive internets, as happened with railroads and highways, and there are already efforts to build the next generation networks to compete with and to improve upon the existing internet [24].

CHAPTER 19

TECHNOLOGY AS PRETEXT

Politicians often speak in code, and technologies often provide the code. Politicians need a language to express policy preferences and make promises to satisfy their immediate and preferred constituents, but without alienating their secondary constituents and the general public. How do you promise a new highway to the business interests in your community without alienating the voters who will be negatively affected by the traffic and the pollution? How do you advocate financial support for families and married couples without alienating single professionals, students, and homosexuals? How do you propose financial aid to rural farmers without drawing the wrath of urban and suburban professionals? Enter technologies that can be used as pretext for political positions [2].

When conservative politicians talk about the brutality of abortion technologies and the science of unborn life, their concern is not so much the science of when life begins, or a technological debate about how to improve abortions to make them less traumatic. Instead, they are taking a political position against those who benefit from abortion technologies, and for those who are disadvantaged by them. That political debate is between the professional women who benefit from the sexual freedom provided by the abortion technologies, and the homemakers whose livelihood is threatened by the advantages gained by those professional women. Technology of abortion and the science of life in womb merely provide a pretext for that political debate [19].

When liberal politicians talk about rape, they do not typically mean a violent assault by a stranger, which is rare. Instead, they increasingly mean statutory rape which is consensual sex with a minor, typically a teenager, or they mean date rape which is consensual sex which went wrong, or they mean marital rape which is a consensual relationship that turned into a conflict. In all of these cases, rape has become a code word for a political struggle. It is a political position against teenagers who would like to compete sexually with adults, or against men who would like to have more sexual power and rights in their relationships. The political struggle has little to do with rape, but a lot to do with a power struggle within sexual relationships. If rape was only about violence, then there would actually be little need for specific laws and prohibitions, since the laws against assault, kidnapping, and unlawful restraint would cover those cases. Adding to the struggle is the legitimate fear of women that they may never be able to prove criminality in a private act, because there are no witnesses, and often no physical evidence. In some traditional societies, the charge of rape is always accepted prima facie as truth, solely on the belief that women would not lie about such a shameful act, and that is a formidable source of power for women. But in societies where rape is not considered such a devastating and total destruction of a woman's social value, that formidable power was also degraded, leading to the current political struggle. Technologies of modern birth control created this dilemma, by empowering women to have sexual freedom outside of reproductive sex, but at the same time taking away the absolute power they had in protecting themselves from unwanted sex, since an active sex life with many partners necessarily blurs the distinction between wanted and unwanted sex, by creating a spectrum of various degrees of consent, short of a written and notarized contract ahead of time detailing the nature, time, and place of sexual activity [9].

Similarly, when politicians talk about pedophilia, they rarely mean actual psychiatric condition of pedophilia, but often they mean teenage sex. Actual pedophilia as a psychiatric condition involves sex with children under 8 and it is very rare. Teenage sex on the other hand is very common, and poses a real threat to adults. Teenagers pose a significant threat of sexual competition to adults, especially because they tend to be hedonistic and sensual, as opposed to adult relationships which tend to be more negotiating and contractual, partly because teenagers are not yet financially independent, and they don't see relationships as long term financial contracts. Furthermore, access to birth control and peer-to-peer communication systems such as cell phones and social networks made teenagers increasingly empowered, and increasingly able to challenge the power of their parents over their sex lives. Parents are always threatened by their children's sexuality, because it diverts the children's love and affection away from their parents, and threatens their monopoly over their children's love and affection. That is why it is a constant source of friction between parents and their teenage children, but only to the extent that teenagers are empowered by technologies to mount a challenge [17]

When conservative politicians talk about small government, they do not mean less military, less police, less surveillance, or fewer laws controlling marriage, sex, and private lives of citizens; but they mean less welfare, less social security, less public infrastructure, and less public education. "Small government" as a code word is not about a smaller government, but a political position directing the government spending towards the interests of the wealthy and the privileged, and away from the poor and the disadvantaged. Modern mass communications crated the need for such coded messages that convey different meanings for different constituencies, because the message is distributed widely [2].

When liberal politicians talk about sex trafficking, they rarely mean enslavement of women into prostitution, but increasingly they are taking a political position against voluntary prostitution. Sex trafficking and enslavement are rare in the US, and when it happens, the legal penalties for forced enslavement are very harsh, so the issue is not stiffer penalties for enslavement. Prostitution on the other hand has become increasingly acceptable as a right for women, as part of the philosophy that values individual autonomy and ownership of one's own body. It is that acceptance that threatens entrenched interests by cheapening the value of women's sexuality and making it widely available. Access to birth control technologies, medical treatments for infections with antibiotics, and distributed communication technologies such as cell phones, web sites, and social media to search for and locate potential sex partners, all together made prostitution a viable source of income for many women, allowing even some college students and single mothers to engage in it part time. And that kind of broad availability of sex, and the resulting price competition, is the real political threat to the high value of women's sexuality. It is a significant economic threat to those who benefit from the noncompetitive high price of sex, such as full time homemakers, and to those who already committed to paying that high price, such as men married to full time homemakers [9].

Sometimes, the coded message sounds silly and incoherent to those who are not privy to the underlying code and interpret the message literally. Representative Todd Akin of Missouri said during the 2012 elections that rape does not cause pregnancy, which led to wide spread ridicule and outright shock, because the general public missed the underlying code to correctly interpret the message. What he meant to say is a complex set of political arguments that have been made by many conservative politicians. First, rape rarely leads to pregnancy in the US, because the rape victims are treated with anti-pregnancy drugs in hospital emergency rooms. Second, there is some evidence that the female body has some minimal resistance to pregnancy when sex is forced and unpleasant. The evidence comes from the studies of female orgasm that suggest that orgasmic muscle spasms facilitate pregnancy by moving the sperm upstream; and the assumption is that the opposite must be true to some extent when there is no orgasm. Further evidence comes from the studies of duck female genitalia that can provide considerable resistance to pregnancy, by routing the sperm to dead end tubes within the vagina, instead of the fallopian tube containing the female egg. Most important part of the message is not the scientific evidence, but the political message that, irrespective of any scientific evidence, rape should not be used as an excuse for terminating pregnancy. The concern is that if rape is made an exception to any ban on abortions, then anybody who wants an abortion could claim rape to get an abortion, and that would render any ban ineffectual. Those who are privy to the code of the abortion debate understood his message, but the rest of the population was befuddled. The argument for such elaborate coding is most obvious when one realizes that he could not state such an elaborate argument explicitly, not only because of its complexity, but also because it would alienate a large block of voters, sexually active women, who would like to take their claims of rape taken seriously, even when it is not violent, because it is a significant source of power to be able to accuse others of criminal behavior in a private act, and have a lighter burden of proof than other criminal acts. Add to it the legitimate fear of women that they may never be able to prove criminality in a private act, since there are no witnesses, and often no physical evidence, and you have a serious political struggle [18].

CHAPTER 20
TECHNOLOGIES OF TRUST AND COMPROMISE

Political campaigns are advertising campaigns where the product is a political candidate and buyers are the voters. A political campaign is an effort to establish trust in a candidate in terms of his future behavior as a leader in exercising delegated power. Voters have to decide whether that future behavior is likely to be consistent with their own self-interest. Establishing trust is accomplished through an advertising model where the candidates sell themselves as products through rallies, speeches, and television appearances, to lay out their philosophy of governance, their way of thinking and decision making, their political priorities, and their personal qualities. But advertising is a faulty model for establishing trust! Relying on sellers as a source of information to guide the behavior of buyers' decisions is a faulty model because the sellers have an incentive to distort their messages to sell their products to the largest possible segment of the population. That incentive leads to unreliable information in two different ways:

a. Information may be tailored to each audience to create the impression of compatibility and trustworthiness with many disparate and mutually incompatible groups.

b. Information may be left vague or coded, to create the impression that the product or the candidate is compatible with and trustworthy to many, when in fact a more specific description of the product would limit its appeal more narrowly. Such coding of information became an art, as the former governor of New York, Mario Cuomo, put it: "You campaign in poetry; but you govern in prose" [2].

Multiple products or candidates doing the same kind of distortion and coding, in favor of their own messages, while undermining others' messages, does not lead to the discovery of truth. Many distorted messages does not equal one reliable and trustworthy message. This problem is endemic to all adversarial systems from advertising and politics, to news analysis and legislation. This problem was created by mass communication systems that allowed sellers to blanket and dominate the media and control the information received by the buyers. Before mass communication technologies, buyers relied on their personal networks for reliable information and recommendations [25].

Electronic social networks create an opportunity to return to an earlier model of information dissemination, by propagating through networks, rather than direct broadcasting to the masses. There are four approaches to accomplishing this objective, in increasing level of sophistication:

a. Mass dissemination of information can simply be replaced with personalized dissemination through a network of trusted partners. This is similar to viral dissemination of popular videos and photos on social networks like Facebook. Each person is connected to its trusted partners, and the information travels by each person posting it to its partners. The popularity of viral videos and twitter feeds is a testament to the effectiveness of such a peer-to-peer propagation [10].

b. In a more sophisticated network, individuals can assign weights to their trusted partners, indicating the level of trust, so that they can restrict the amount of information they receive, and control the quality. They can limit their information intake to messages with a certain level of trust, computed by aggregating the trust levels of all the partners approving that message, and possibly by subtracting the trust levels of all those disapproving the message. Alternatively, all messages from trusted partners are received, but they are ranked and prioritized according to the total trust value attached to each.

A variation on this approach is to create a global trust value for each piece of information, product, or service, by aggregating the trust values attached to that piece by all raters, but also by weighting each trust value by the trustworthiness of the rater. The trustworthiness of the rater is also established in the same fashion recursively, by aggregating all the trust values it received, themselves weighted by the trustworthiness of the raters. Such recursive definitions are common in Computer science, and Google's Web Search Engine works like this.

Google's famous Page Rank search algorithm uses links incoming to a webpage as votes of trust, and simply counts them to calculate the total trust on that page, but it also weights each link according to the trustworthiness of its source, recursively defined in the same manner, by counting its incoming links, and weighting hem according to their source, ad infinatum [7].

This method has considerable potential in evaluating the trustworthiness of all information from movie and restaurant recommendations, to judging the quality of academic papers to finding a reliable doctor. Such peer-to-peer evaluation maybe most effective in judging the quality of professional services, and the electronic social networks can accomplish this efficiently in very large scale. The evaluation of academic articles for example can be accomplished without an infrastructure of journals, editors, publishers, and reviewers. Articles can be self-published into digital repositories, and rated by all readers. Then an evaluation scheme, similar to Google's Page Rank, can easily aggregate all those ratings, weighted by the trustworthiness and the professional standing of those raters. The trustworthiness of the reviewers is similarly computed by aggregating the ratings they received, themselves weighted by the trustworthiness of the raters. Such recursive definitions have proven to be very effective in Search Engines. Furthermore, incentives can be devised to encourage more reviews and to improve the quality of reviews, by linking the trustworthiness of reviewers to the quality and the quantity of the reviews they submit, and the quality of the reviews themselves are determined recursively by the ratings they receive weighted by the trustworthiness of the raters. In effect, everything is rated recursively by everything else. Such a system can greatly reduce the cost, and increase the speed of academic publishing, and significantly improve the quality of reviews by aggregating them over larger samples than currently possible [7].

c. The next level of sophistication and complexity involves complete delegation of some decisions to trusted partners. Once you establish the trustworthiness of an agent from their previous interactions with you, or with your trusted partners, or transitively with their trusted partners, following the network connections to arbitrary depth, then you can safely delegate some decisions to trustworthy agents. This is where both economic and political decision making can be drastically altered and improved. The approach would be similar to delegating medical decisions to your doctor, or legal decisions to your lawyer, since clearly they have specialized knowledge and they are better equipped to make decisions on your behalf than you could; and you have established trust with them through a mechanism of professional certification, recommendations from others you trust, and your own past experiences with them. This informal process of establishing trust can be replaced with a more formal and elaborate system relying on electronic social networks, where you can aggregate recommendations and ratings from a much larger set of trusted partners and their trusted partners, and you can weight them according to the reliability of the source, and delegate only if the aggregate trust level exceeds a predetermined threshold. All professional credentials received, all accolades and reprimands conferred by professional organizations, and all evaluations and ratings by peers, are automatically included since they are all trusted agents in the system. All agents have incentives to provide correct ratings and evaluations, since their own trustworthiness depends on the quality of the ratings and recommendations they provided in the past. Incentives can be expanded by devising payment systems to remunerate trusted partners for their services in proportion to the utilization of their ratings and recommendations, and the utilization itself depends on the quality and the quantity of services they provided in the past [20].

d. Delegation does not have to be full. One could delegate decisions partially, or to a set of agents collectively. Partial delegation can be accomplished by delegating each agent a part of a decision, or delegating a decision to different agents under different conditions. For example, a medical decision can be delegated to one doctor if the illness is terminal and end of life decisions have to be made and to another doctor if the illness is not life threatening; or the surgical and pharmaceutical parts of a treatment decision can be delegated to different doctors.

Collective delegation can be accomplished by delegating a medical decision to a group of medical doctors, but only if they can reach a consensus, or follow the majority opinion [20].

Imagine electronic communities where consumption decisions are made collectively, as a result of some political process. For example, all community members purchase an item if a consensus is reached, or none does. This involves delegation of an otherwise individual consumption decision to the group. Some group purchasing communities like Groupon have such features. Imagine a public taxation system where individuals can direct their taxes partially or fully to specific government projects they trust; or direct their votes to trusted partners who in turn can direct their taxes to specific government projects for them, or vote for specific political candidates for them. This can be accomplished by joining a variety of electronic communities and allocating some of your taxes to those communities, then the community can vote collectively on various public issues or fund various government projects on behalf of its members. Communities may reach decisions through internal deliberations, or they may delegate their votes to a community leader for a period of time, who may in turn makes economic, political, and social decisions for the whole group. Such delegation may create considerable political power since the leader is empowered to speak for the whole group.

Such a system of delegation is considerably different from the current representative democracies where the power is also delegated to elected representatives, because under this system the delegation of power can involve many communities, each trusted in a very narrow context. That can lead to a more enlightened political process, since the community leaders can develop expertise and become quite knowledgeable each in a very narrow context, yet wield considerable power in representing a large community in that narrow context. That would be similar to what lobbyists, local community leaders, and influential journalists do now informally; but can be formalized with actual delegated power, and developed in much larger scale over electronic social networks. They can also be extended to multiple levels of delegation ranging from local communities like school boards, to national communities like labor unions, to even international communities like human rights groups, depending on the scope of the issue at hand. Such multi-level structures can be organized hierarchically to accommodate increasingly narrow contexts, and for consistent delegation and aggregation of power in those contexts. Such multi-level and narrowly targeted delegation systems have the potential to drastically change currently existing political systems, for two reasons. First, they convert an existing one or two level representative hierarchy into a multi-level hierarchy; and second, they convert the existing comprehensive delegation systems where political power is not dependent on context or issue, to a partial delegation system where each leader's delegated power is context-specific. For example, a representative may be able to vote on your behalf only on foreign policy issues, and another may represent your interests only on domestic infrastructure decisions, and each leader may represent varying numbers of people ranging from a handful to millions depending on the community structure and determined through a hierarchy of trust levels. Such flexibility in representation would lead to a distributed democracy with widely diffused power, and it would lead to distributed decision making at multiple levels of granularity while keeping them consistent through partial delegation [20].

PART 5
A PROPOSAL FOR SOCIAL ENGINEERING

People specialize in designing cars, planes, or computers; but nobody specializes in designing families, religions, or governments. Are they not as important?

A technology-driven society is a society in constant flux and subject to accelerating change. In that environment, traditions and cultural values become obsolete at an increasing rate, and lose their value as inter-generational learning tools. Social institutions become obsolete faster than they could be modified; and when they are modified, intense global competition favors short-term advantages, leaving little opportunity to develop complex social structures with long-term advantages. Markets become the dominant cure to treat all social problems. To solve these problems, a proposal for an interdisciplinary field of study called "social engineering" is sketched out. The proposal involves comprehensive theories of interaction between technologies and social structures; and an extensive regime of experimentation with alternative technologies and alternative social institutions. Experiments are expected to rely on modern communication and coordination technologies; and they are expected to be protected from short-term competition from established technologies and traditional social institutions for long periods of time, to allow them to develop, and eventually to compete.

CHAPTER 21
TECHNOLOGY

Technology is different from science. Science aims to explain the world around us; technology aims to change it. As such, those who create technology do so explicitly to change the world, and they always face a design question as to what type of world is desired [2, 3]. Unfortunately, the long term impact of technologies is very poorly understood, and technology creators rarely consider them. Technology creators aim to solve immediate problems, using short-term cost-benefit analysis, and typically ignore the long-term consequences. The reasons for such short-sightedness are partly the difficulty of predicting long-term consequences, and partly the lack of incentives to consider them. Long-term consequences are difficult to predict because there are long chains of cause and effect, with multiple interacting factors at each step. There are no incentives to consider these long-term consequences because they are not clearly linked to the technologies, and even when they are, the creators get neither praise nor blame for them. Worse yet, because of the difficulty of prediction, and the lack of incentives, no learning takes place. Even after the consequences are realized, any learning and analysis is reactive to the past technologies, not proactive towards the forthcoming technologies. With little or no learning taking place, technologies continue to impact society and the environment in a completely unpredicted, unplanned, and uncontrolled fashion [25, 28].

Consider the automobile technology. It was designed and promoted as the "clean" technology, to remedy the pollution caused by the earlier horse and buggy technology. The automobile certainly remedied the problem of filthy and smelly streets; but the pollution problems it created were completely unpredicted and unplanned. Similarly, the new clean technologies such as solar and wind power are designed to remedy the immediate environmental problems, but their long-term impact on the environment is not known or even seriously investigated [1].

As unplanned as it is, the social impact of technologies is often dramatic and critically important. Technology, more than anything else, determines the human condition. Humans have distinguished themselves from all other species in their keen ability to create complex tools, and use them to modify their environment. Moreover, the desire to take maximum advantage of a technology often requires a reorganization of the human society, which creates new opportunities and imperatives to create new technologies, leading to an unending cycle. As such, technology and organization are the two inseparable components of the same basic human endeavor. Tools are created to change the environment to fit the human needs; the society is reorganized to take maximum advantage of the new tools and the modified environment; the new organization creates new human needs and consequently a need for new tools to further modify the environment. Past experience suggests that this cycle is not likely to converge, because the new technologies and the new organizations are designed to solve short-term problems, and their long-term consequences are often maladaptive, feeding or even accelerating the cycle. In fact, the cycle has been accelerating throughout human history, with the faster development of new technologies, and faster (yet increasingly inadequate) pace of adaptation by human organizations and institutions to the faster technology development cycle [5, 9].

Consider again the transportation technologies. They resulted in a mobile society where fewer and fewer people reside with their extended families, or live permanently in their place of birth. That led to an increasing demand for communication technologies to keep them connected. Mail, telegraph, telephone, and internet are all responses to that need created by a previous generation of technologies that made the society more mobile. Telephone or internet in a pre-industrial society would have been an enigma, satisfying no particular need, real or imagined. Similarly, smaller and eventually nuclear families with only two adults are also the result of an increasingly mobile society, where large extended families are a burden, restricting economic opportunities created by mobility. This trend is accelerating, with average household size in the US dipping below two adults for the first time, with a large number of adults living alone, and many with no children. Yet, humans did not evolve to live in such small families, but in larger groups of 15-30 like all other apes. Such social consequences of transportation technologies were not anticipated, let alone planned for, at the time of development and introduction of these technologies [15, 24, 29].

CHAPTER 22
DISCONTENT

It is difficult to overstate the importance of the interaction between technology and society. Yet, our understanding is minimal, and it is almost always ex post facto, benefitting from hindsight. We analyze and study what various technologies have done to our societies, after the fact, and resign to the unpredictability of technologies and their social impact, before we create them. We create technologies to solve immediate problems, and deal with the long-term consequences incrementally, and as they appear. There are numerous problems with this approach [18].

First, if the consequences are undesirable, it is difficult to reverse them by discontinuing the use of the technology, because the effects may persist after the discontinuation, and even be permanent. Consider global warming. There is widespread agreement that global warming is likely to continue for some time, because of the persistence of the high concentrations of CO_2 in the atmosphere, even if we could reduce or even eliminate the use of fossil fuels.

Second, if the consequences are undesirable, it may be difficult to discontinue the use of a technology, because many secondary technologies and social institutions may have been created around the technology. In fact, completely new lifestyles may have developed around new technologies and the resulting social institutions. Once a technology leads to a new lifestyle, technology and the lifestyle reinforce each other, and they become very difficult to retract. Lifestyles and cultural norms are notoriously difficult to change, because they are designed to provide stability and permanence. They also create political and social advantages for some groups over others, and that engenders political realities that are difficult to reverse. Reversing them may lead to major social disruptions and dislocations. Consider the suburbs, and the suburban life style. They were created to take advantage of the mobility created by the automobile technology. Once created, the suburbs reinforced the dependence on the automobile, and made them an indispensable part of modern life. Eliminating the urban-suburban lifestyle would require abandoning major investments in infrastructure, and reversing major social and psychological commitments to many cultural norms about family life and child rearing. Consider birth control and abortion technologies. Completely new lifestyles involving sexual freedom and professionalization of women were created by these technologies. Attempts to reverse these social adjustments would be very difficult, as evidenced by unending culture wars. Women's professionalization for example created a professional class of women who gained economic and social advantages over traditional homemakers, and that advantage would be difficult to give up, even if the technologies that led to it may prove to be undesirable for any reason [5, 15].

Third, even if it is possible for a technology to be withdrawn from use, and the social adjustments to be reversed, there may be no incentive for any group to discontinue use unilaterally, and collective action may be difficult to achieve, especially if the technology provides short-term advantages to those who defect from the collective action. Consider the invention of flint-stone spearheads by hunter-gatherer humans. A spearhead had a huge survival advantage because it allowed humans to hunt big game animals for the first time in human history, by allowing them to hunt from a throwing distance. Yet, the technology over time led to a population explosion because of the sudden abundance of a high-protein food source, and it encouraged warfare because of both the population explosion and the adoption of the technology to warfare itself. Spearheads made warfare extremely bloody and impersonal, fought from a distance, and the investment into and development of spearheads started dominating the economic lives of hunter-gatherer tribes. Yet, the technology could not simply be withdrawn or discontinued through any disarmament agreement, when it provided such decisive short-term advantages. Many millennia later, war ships, fighter jets, nuclear arms, and remote controlled drones all followed the same pattern [7, 26].

Fourth, incrementally optimum changes in technologies do not necessarily lead to a long-term globally optimum outcome. In fact, it is possible to get into a vicious cycle where each incrementally optimum change can trigger many other changes, and while each one alone is optimum at the time, their totality may lead to consistently worse outcomes over time. Classic examples of vicious cycles are arms races, or blood feuds, where each action responding to the other's transgression is optimal, yet the outcome at each step is increasing expenditures into arms on both sides, with no relative advantage, or increasing loss of life on both sides, with no apparent victory. The same pattern can be observed in our modern reliance on synthetic chemicals to improve our lives. Each new synthetic chemical we create solves an immediate problem in agriculture, medicine, manufacturing, or home maintenance, but may create long-term environmental and health hazards. To solve the environmental and health problems, we create more synthetic chemicals, leading potentially to even more environmental and health problems. More critically, each new synthetic chemical introduces some very small risk of catastrophic environmental consequences, and that risk multiplies with every new chemical we introduce, especially because combinations of chemicals in the environment can have a drastically different impact than each one alone. The accelerating rate of introduction of new chemicals into the environment, which is currently about seven thousand a year, multiplies the risk indefinitely, eventually leading to an unacceptably high probability of catastrophic consequences [27, 29].

Social adjustments to technologies can reinforce such vicious cycles. Synthetic fertilizers were welcome by the world to feed "a billion hungry mouths". Synthetic fertilizers made food cheap and easily accessible, and the world's poor responded enthusiastically by having more children. Many decades after the introduction of synthetic fertilizers, we still have "a billion hungry mouths"; and new synthetic chemicals and genetically modified agricultural products are being advocated as the solution, with unknown long-term consequences for the environment. Such vicious cycles are very common in social adjustments to new technologies. Consider the nuclear family. It creates severe emotional dependence on partners since two adults living as a unit isolated from the extended family is rather new in human history. Such emotional dependence creates high expectations, makes marriages fragile, and leads to high rates of divorce. Fragile marriages make people even more severely dependent on that one partner, putting additional pressure on marriages. This vicious cycle can only be avoided by returning to large families in which humans evolved, where the emotional energy is distributed over many loved ones; but the mobility requirements of modern societies dominated by transportation technologies makes that impossible [1, 5].

Similarly, antibiotics were considered miracle drugs that cured humanity's most dreaded ailments such as tuberculosis and leprosy. But availability of antibiotics also encouraged a social adjustment, leading to a completely different kind of industrial animal farming, where animals are crowded into unsanitary and unhealthy pens, and kept alive simply by administering large doses of antibiotics. This kind of farming produced cheap food for billions, and allowed sharp rises in population, but it also led to mutations in bacteria, and development of antibiotic resistant bacteria. Now, about 90,000 patients a year in the US alone die from infections with antibiotic resistant bacteria. Tuberculosis is back with a vengeance killing 2 million people a year world-wide. Of course, these setbacks only encourage the development of new antibiotics, and subsequently new social adjustments, using even more drugs in humans and farm animals, completing the cycle. These cycles are very difficult to break, because social adjustments create dependencies, change the social structure and traditions, and even the complete lifestyles. One cannot simply stop using antibiotics, without reverting to an earlier mode of farming. Earlier modes of farming cannot support the existing population and its urban lifestyle, without condemning a large segment of the human population to starvation [16].

There are three broad categories of solutions proposed for these problems:

a. The optimistic solution denies the problem and advocates an unplanned incremental approach. It relies on human ingenuity to solve problems as they occur, with increasingly faster technological developments. The risk of man-made catastrophes is minimized compared to natural catastrophes that are not under human control. Markets are idolized, and unplanned uncontrolled rush into the future is depicted as progress. The fact that optimum long-term outcome may not be achieved is not considered a problem, since planning and predicting the future may be impossible anyway. The advocates of this approach tend to shun planning and regulation. They favor unregulated market mechanisms introducing and supporting new technologies, and if they lead to occasional environmental, social, or economic crises, that is the price to pay for efficiencies created by markets. This solution underestimates the risks [22].

b. The pessimistic solution argues that such unplanned and unpredicted changes in technology, environments, and society are non-sustainable. Risk of catastrophes goes up over time, and exponentially. Even without catastrophes, the human society is likely to experience a decline in the quality of life, due to increasing resources and energy devoted to remedying the unexpected consequences of technologies. The solution proposed here is to get off the roller coaster, stop the reliance on technology, and return to a pre-industrial life-style. This solution underestimates the difficulty of drastically changing our social structures and lifestyles, without creating extreme disruption, instability, and even warfare among the constituents who will be disparately affected by the changes [28].

c. A third and an intermediate approach is taken by the environmental and sustainability movements. It advocates slowing down the introduction of new technologies through government action, testing and regulating them more carefully, and encouraging technologies that may be more sustainable. This approach does not change the underlying dynamic of technology introduction and unintended consequences, but slows it down, reduces risk, and delays potentially catastrophic consequences [1, 9]. This approach overestimates our ability to test and predict.

Remember that automobile technology was introduced as "the clean technology". We often do not know the long-term consequences of "sustainable" technologies. They may not turn out to be the clean technologies we envision them to be. Mass production of solar technology might turn out to be as dirty as the automobile technology. As the early automobile technology focused on dirty streets, they missed the possibility of dirty air. As we focus on the lack of air pollution from solar energy production, we may be missing the environmental costs of the solar panel manufacturing, or some other factor such as eventual scarcity of sun exposed space.

A fundamental solution to the ad-hoc development and introduction of technologies has to accomplish two things:

a. Prediction: There must be reliable and sound methodologies to predict the long-term social and environmental effects of technologies. This would probably require a new interdisciplinary field of study, to classify technologies, for each class to identify the potential social and environmental consequences, and to establish the conditions necessary for each of those consequences to be realized. Extending the analysis over time should produce potential trajectories of technology development, deployment, and adoption, and social adjustment, social entrenchment, and institution building, and finally triggering the development of new secondary technologies, and repeating the cycle. Uncertainty and conditional development should produce large numbers of alternatives at each step, forming a tree of possible trajectories, with probabilities and conditions attached to each step. This kind of analysis is typically practiced in contingency analysis, in military or disaster recovery planning, but rarely tried to predict long term social consequences.

b. Design: For each possible alternate route, escape routes need to be designed with an action plan to mitigate undesirable consequences. The action plan will likely involve the design of new technologies and social institutions to accomplish the mitigation. Moreover, incentives and enforcement mechanisms have to be designed to encourage or even force participation by all relevant parties. These design problems again are similar to contingency planning in military and disaster recovery, but rarely tried in planning for long-term undesirable social consequences of technologies. Such fundamental design solutions require a new interdisciplinary field of study that develops design techniques to create contingent technologies and remedial social institutions to mitigate potential future problems.

We will call this new field of study "Social Engineering" since it undertakes analysis, prediction, and design simultaneously. It involves social sciences in understanding, analyzing, and predicting the social impact of technologies; and it involves engineering and design in intervening in social processes to create desirable social impact, by building and promoting various secondary technologies and social institutions. It provides economic analysis to discover the proper incentives to encourage all parties to cooperate with the planned interventions. It provides political analysis to assess the differential impact of technologies on different constituencies. Finally, it repeats the prediction and intervention steps for each possible trajectory to accommodate uncertainty. These are challenging tasks, especially because the field is expected to be inter-disciplinary, linking such disparate fields as sociology, economics, political science, computer science, and various engineering disciplines, into a cohesive unit.

CHAPTER 23
SOCIAL ENGINEERING

As a first attempt to sketch out the broad parameters of the field of Social Engineering, it is possible to classify technologies and their social impact into four general categories. Further work would need to identify finer categories at multiple levels of aggregation, leading to detailed ontologies.

a. Technologies that extract and store resources: Extraction is the movement of resources from past to present, and storage is the movement of resources from present to future. Agricultural and energy technologies typically extract resources from nature, and store them for future use.

b. Technologies that move resources over space: Transportation technologies typically move resources from where they are extracted and stored to where they are used.

c. Technologies that extract and store information: Science, religion, literature, and art extract information from the world around us by observing, describing, classifying, and analyzing the information we glean from our environment; and books, music, movies, traditions, and cultures store that information for future generations.

d. Technologies that move information over space: Communication technologies from messengers to mail, language to writing, and phone to internet all move information from where it was created and stored to where it is needed and used.

These categories of technologies have typical trajectories they follow in terms of development and social impact, which provide a good starting point for any analysis:

a. Technologies that extract resources lead to capital formation and large scale resource ownership, since any movement of resources over a time period raises the question of who controls it during that time period. Initially, the resource is typically abundant and the extraction processes are simple, and those who extract the resource typically own it and store it. As the resource is depleted and the extraction technologies become more complex, the processes of extraction and storage become more capital intensive, specialized, automated, and outsourced; and the ownership is increasingly separated from labor and concentrated. Complex legal frameworks and social constructs are created to determine and protect ownership rights [10]. Consider agricultural technologies. They led to land and livestock ownership, caused the separation of capital from labor, which is the primary concern of all political and economic institutions to this day. Consider solar energy, which is in its early stages of development, and those who extract it typically own it. But as it follows its expected trajectory, it is likely to lead to increasing ownership of solar energy extracted by others. It is easy to see from plant life where solar energy is the main source of life, the competition takes place mainly in securing a location with consistent sun exposure. Plants compete aggressively for ownership of those locations, but also for the ownership of locations that can block the competitors' sun exposure.

There are two broad approaches to resource ownership. Private ownership leads to concentration of power, since those who own resources have an incentive to join forces and monopolize critical resources, and exploit non-owners. Typical examples are concentration of power in oil and gas industries. Collective ownership on the other hand, leads to excessive utilization of resources, at rates faster than the renewal rate. Since it is difficult to track utilization of collectively owned resources, all participants rush in to exploit the resource before it is depleted. Typical examples are the excessive exploitation and depletion of ocean fish and forest timber. Moreover, vicious cycles can develop where concentration of power and the consequent economic power leads to even more concentration of power; and excessive utilization of resources and the consequent fear of depletion leads to even more excessive utilization [26]. Consider synthetic fertilizer. This technology led to extraction of food from some of the most barren lands. It was justified as there were "a billion hungry mouths" in the world. Yet, as the technology spread and food became more abundant, people in poverty simply had more children, and today there are still "a billion hungry mouths' in the world. Consequently, more wide spread use of synthetic fertilizers, and even newer technologies like genetically modified crops are justified on that basis. Such vicious cycles can develop both with privately owned and collectively owned resources, so our political debates concentrating on ownership do not adequately address these problems. Solutions to such vicious cycles require experimentation with and development of technologies and organizational structures that limit the power created by private ownership, and limit the excessive resource utilization created by collective ownership [12]. We will introduce some solutions in the next section.

b. Technologies that move resources lead to specialization, as they enable the movement of resources to a specialized location for each step in the process of production. Specialization leads to distribution of ownership over time and space, and coordination becomes the dominant issue, since resources are now owned by many participants who cooperate with each other in processing the resources. Consider transportation technologies, and the consequent globalization as a social construct. They led to specialization in agriculture and industry based on competitive advantages in land, climate, natural resources, or labor skills, leading to great global efficiencies, but creating difficult problems in coordination and risk. Global efficiency comes at a cost of increasing need for global communication and coordination, and increasing risk where failure in one location cannot be localized, but impacts the global economy. Furthermore, the increasing need for communication and coordination led to the development of global institutions such as global banks and exchanges, and in the process created even more single points of failure. As a result, crises are increasingly global and all encompassing. Consider the efficiencies crated by the global banking industry. Global movement of capital is critical to the efficient development and processing of resources. But, these efficiencies come at an increasing cost of running a large and global financial system, which is an ever larger component of the global economy. When the efficiency of various markets are computed and exalted, the cost of the financial system necessary to make the markets efficient is almost never considered, and the risk of future global crises is always an afterthought to current global efficiencies [21, 27].

There are two broad approaches to coordination. Centralized coordination requires all decisions to be made at the center, and all information to flow to the center. Decentralized coordination gives each participant considerable autonomy within some generally agreed goals. There are many intermediate approaches. They all have to balance the cost of information processing and information overload at the center, against the cost of incomplete information and incompatibility of decisions in the periphery. To add to the complexity, the movement of resources always challenges the ownership of resources, because those who monopolize resources in one locality cannot prevent competition from other localities, when resources can move easily. Instead, to increase efficiency, they are forced to rely on other specialized resources owned by others. The solutions involve balancing of information overload with incomplete information, and balancing of ownership with movement; and require complex analysis and experimentation. New technologies and organizational structures need to be created to limit complexity and risk of global coordination while taking advantage of the efficiencies created by specialization [27, 30]. We will introduce some solutions in the next section.

c. Technologies that create and store information lead to information capital and large scale ownership of information. They create a professional class of workers who own and control the information capital. They challenge the economic dominance of the physical resource ownership. As in physical resources, these technologies lead to the development of complex legal frameworks and social constructs to determine and protect the ownership rights. Historically the emergence of the "priest and artisan" classes to challenge the economic domination of the "landed aristocracy", and the emergence of "professional and managerial" classes to challenge the "industrial and merchant" classes have both followed this trajectory. Consider religion and science. They extract information about our physical and social environment and store it in books, rituals, music, art, stories, traditions, and recently in electronic media. Institutions such as the church and the university are created to protect the information by storing it faithfully, to preserve its integrity by following complex protocols in extending and modifying it, and to maintain its credibility by limiting the membership authorized to learn and follow those protocols [15].

There are two approaches to the ownership of information resources. Private ownership leads to scarcity of information and concentration of power, since those who own information have an incentive to restrict access to critical information and exploit non-owners. Collective ownership of information leads to excessive production and distribution of less than reliable information to influence and control the behavior of others to further one's own interests. Consider professional organizations. They routinely restrict access to the professions and the private body of knowledge they control, ostensibly to maintain quality, but also to limit competition. You can't practice law, medicine or accounting without accreditation from a professional organization. Churches and universities also carefully control admission into their hierarchies. Scientists and priests are often the sole intermediaries between the general public and the impenetrable and incomprehensible body of knowledge and wisdom they possess. University admission has as much to do with limiting access to that knowledge, as it does with the ability to perform. Church rituals have as much to do with inspiring awe and respect in those who have the knowledge and authority to perform them, as it does with providing worship services [5, 15].

On the other hand, collectively owned information such as political opinion, public art, and commercial advertising is often low quality and misleading; and they are produced in large quantities to influence and control public behavior, leading to information overload. Almost all political and commercial information distorts the truth to serve someone's interest. In adversarial systems, truth is nobody's friend, as all parties attempt to distort the facts in their direction to win arguments; and many distorted facts in all directions do not necessarily lead to the discovery of truth. Just because the truth is somewhere in the middle of all arguments does not mean it can be easily found, as evidenced by unending culture wars, where all parties believe a distorted version of truth that serves their political interests. More importantly, social institutions often codify private information into public rules, traditions, and cultures to reinforce their institutional power and influence. But then those rules are very difficult to change as technologies change our environment; and in a fast changing technological society, most institutional rules tend to be obsolete at any given time [28]. Consider the tradition in western societies that women marry a man slightly older than themselves, which is typically 2 years. That tradition is a result of girls sexually maturing earlier than boys, and marrying in their early teens. The tradition is quite obsolete when the average marriage age is late 20's, sexuality is not exclusively within marriage, and women tend to live 8 years longer than men! Similarly obsolete traditions dominate all of our social institutions such as religion, school, and marriage. Fundamental solutions are needed to remedy both the information scarcity created by private ownership, and also the information overload and distortion created by public ownership [5, 28].

d. Technologies that move information over space lead to specialization of knowledge, the distribution and spread of ideas, cultures and social movements, and adding value by building on others' knowledge. They challenge the power of local information monopolists, and age-old traditions and cultures. Such challenges lead to new ideas, but at the cost of instability, cultural conflict, and even culture wars [17, 30]. Consider printing press and books. They undermined the power of the church in Europe, by allowing access to new sources of information by the masses, and thus empowering some new voices ranging from new religious sects to new scientific approaches to discovering truth [21].

There are two approaches to distribution of information. Centralized control of distribution leads to homogenization and globalization of culture, and wide spread adoption of dominant ideas. It creates winner-take-all markets, because distribution breaks down local protections, and exposes all to a global competition of ideas and cultures [23]. Recording of music led to global stars since the distribution was controlled by powerful music labels. Printing of Bible led to spread of Christianity as a global religion practiced in all continents, since the distribution was controlled by powerful churches and missionary organizations. Hollywood movies spread the western culture to far corners of the world, since movie distribution was controlled by major studios.

Decentralized control of distribution, on the other hand, leads to proliferation of ideas, poor quality control, and information overload [6, 17, 19]. Proliferation of printing presses and later communication technologies like radio and television led to the development of many religious sects each slightly different from the next. Internet and the social media led to the proliferation of political ideas and social movements, and challenged the state control of political information from China to Egypt, leading to a variety of challenges to state authority. Cable television and later, social media, led to proliferation of social and sexual attitudes, and led to wide spread challenge by teenagers of their parents' authority over their social and sexual lives. Fundamental solutions are needed to remedy both the homogenization and globalization of culture created by central distribution, and also the information overload and poor quality control created by decentralized distribution.

CHAPTER 24
SOLUTIONS

A field of study that specializes in predicting the social impact of technologies, and designing interventions to prevent undesirable consequences, has considerable potential. It could advance some technologies over others on the basis of anticipated social impact. It could suggest modifications or secondary technologies to alleviate the negative impact and accentuate the positive impact. It could design and promote social adjustments and new social institutions to take maximum advantage of new technologies, or to blunt their negative impact. The field can accomplish these goals by developing theoretical models of how technologies interact with social structures, by testing those theories empirically, and by developing design methodologies for creating new technologies or modifying existing technologies on the basis of their anticipated social impact.

There are numerous problems to overcome in such a field of study. First, comprehensive theories on the interaction of technologies and social structures are not readily available. Second, it is difficult to test such theories empirically, because the causal chains can be very long extending over decades, and they are often multi-faceted with numerous technologies and social structures interacting in complex combinations. Third, it is difficult to run social experiments with alternative technologies and social structures over long periods of time, since these experiments would require complex legal and social frameworks to protect the participants and enforce the rules. Fourth, designing technologies for better social outcomes would invariably require some tradeoff between immediate and long-term benefits. It is difficult to enforce such tradeoffs, since in the market place short-term benefits tend to dominate, especially if long-term benefits are uncertain and difficult to appropriate.

We have sketched out a first step at developing a comprehensive theory of how technologies and social structures interact in Chapter 22. Much more refined theories about specific technologies and their interaction with specific social structures and institutions would be necessary. But, a more fundamental problem is how to test these theories empirically. Historical surveys might be helpful, but collecting reliable data for decades, to track the evolution of a technology and its social context would be difficult. Adding to the difficulty, is the global culture where successful technologies spread very quickly, and the alternatives are destroyed, in the fierce economic competition of global winner-take-all markets. Any long-term comparative analysis is rendered impossible when short-term competition is fierce and global. Yet, experimentation with alternative technologies and social structures over long periods of time would be critical to testing such theories. Such difficulty with experimentation is not unique to this domain, but all social theories suffer from lack of experimentation with social structures.

Ironically, such social experimentation has been the mainstay of human existence for millennia, and provided the basis of most human learning before the modern scientific age. This was accomplished through the concept of "culture", and the simultaneous existence of many diverse cultures for long periods of time. Each culture adopted different technologies and social institutions in relative isolation. That created the possibility of comparing and contrasting cultures, since in the long run, when cultures eventually came into contact, they competed against each other through migration, trade, political action, and warfare to establish the advantages of each. Two components of such cultural competition are critically important: Relative isolation of cultures is important to develop a culture so that short-term advantages do not dominate the long-term advantages. Competition among cultures is important so that members can compare and contrast, and the cultures with superior characteristics can win out and expand [13, 14].

Unfortunately, these two components are in conflict. Increasing isolation means less competition, and less opportunity to compare and contrast cultures. Decreasing isolation creates too much competition among cultures that leads to increasing emphasis on short-term advantages, and no opportunity for a culture to develop fully to reach its long-term potential. Finding a balance between the two components is critical. Unfortunately, modern transportation and communication technologies have moved us towards a mono-cultural world where new technologies and social movements spread rapidly throughout the world, and no culture is isolated enough to adopt alternative technologies and lifestyles long enough to test long-term effects and provide long-term comparison. Current global community makes it difficult to protect cultures and economies long enough to reach maturity and establish their value and advantages. That is why protectionist countries have done well economically, and isolated communities are receiving new attention to protect cultural diversity [4]. Consider the success of the Asian economies. Japan, Korea, and China all developed under serious protectionist measures. Even the US economy developed in the 19th century, by relying on protectionist measures against the United Kingdom and the other well developed economies of the time [4]. Similarly, Native American communities and Asian religious minorities are receiving increasing attention for their contributions to the diversity of cultures.

Striking a balance between protection and competition between cultures is not easy, and despite the rhetoric of protection, the world is moving headlong towards a mono-cultural society. A comprehensive solution to this dilemma would require a number of basic building blocks:

a. Reliable theories are needed to predict the social impact of technologies, as sketched out in Chapter 22.

b. A mechanism is needed to design alternate technologies with different social outcomes.

c. Institutions are needed to encourage the development of communities adopting alternate technologies and building alternate social and political institutions, to create alternative trajectories.

d. Research methodologies are needed to compare and contrast alternative communities, and evaluate their merits and disadvantages.

e. Alternative communities need to be protected from short term competition by isolating them, and allowing them to develop to their full potential. Communities should be able to close themselves, and block social, economic, and political competition for predetermined periods of time.

f. Alternative communities need to be exposed to competition over the long term to encourage learning. Communities would have to compete with each other for members and resources at the termination of various protection periods, to allow communities to develop, yet to freely compete at the end of a development period. No community should be allowed to remain protected indefinitely, to avoid rewarding inferiority.

g. A global organization is needed to regulate communities, and to create and enforce the rules under which communities interact with each other. Such a global organization has to have enforcement power to prevent communities from exploiting their members or each other, using deceit or force to control and lock in their members, or permanently avoiding competition with other communities.

Consider the automobile technology, and the Amish community that rejects that technology. To develop such a community as a viable alternative to the mainstream, Amish need to be protected from social, political, and economic competition, and certainly from outright hostility and violence. They need to be able to close their community, restrict their members to social and economic activities within the community, and manage their community without legal and economic interference from the outside world. Yet, they need to be forced into competition with the outside world periodically, to enable learning by comparing and contrasting cultures. This could be accomplished by opening the community up for free flow of members into and out of the community at pre-determined periods. This argument also applies to many unpopular cult-type communities. They may be much more valuable than we acknowledge, for their willingness to experiment with many unpopular social arrangements. Communities openly competing for membership create competition; but limiting them to predetermined periods prevents short-term competition, and allows them to develop. Currently, very few nation states allow any reasonably free flow of its citizens across the national borders. That exacerbates the ongoing struggle between capital and labor, since capital can flow rather freely over the national borders, to nations where labor is cheap and unorganized; but labor cannot easily move into nations where labor is expensive and organized [23].

Some experimental communities can be created as online experiments. Online communities with their own social, political, and ethical arrangements can be quite useful to determine the potential of new social structures without undue risk to the participants. But online experimentation has its limits, especially if it reduces the risk to participants by avoiding direct contact with other humans, and then can only work as an initial screening device for new social arrangements. The behavior of participants in any experiment can be drastically different if the environment is perceived as contrived and riskless, as opposed to real and costly. Realistic experimentation may require physical experimental communities. Forming, managing, and protecting such communities are communication and coordination intensive, and may require extensive support from communication and coordination technologies themselves. At some point, the distinction between online communities and physical communities tends to blur, since technology and physical contact are both needed to conduct such experiments in realistic settings with convincing results [8, 19].

Consider a government taxation system that allows taxpayers to direct their payments to specific government projects; or even a completely voluntary taxation system which relies on transparency alone, where the payments by each citizen and its impact on the general welfare is computed and publicized. Such experiments can be conducted easily in online communities that use taxation for specific community organizations. Once a proof of concept is demonstrated, it can be made available to various physical communities ranging from sports clubs to municipalities for adoption for specific time periods. Such communities should be protected from competition as they work out the details, and should be rewarded for providing a valuable service to others by taking the risk of experimenting with alternatives. At the end of trial periods, such communities should be opened up to competition, by allowing members to join or leave such communities in preference for other communities. Other communities themselves may observe the outcome of these experiments, and imitate or join the successful communities. Such experimentation can be a very productive tool of social learning in a fast-changing technology-driven environment, where traditions are becoming obsolete at an accelerating rate [8, 20].

Consider a peer-to-peer banking system where loans are channeled through trusted peers from lenders to borrowers. Such a distributed banking system can provide a serious challenge to the current centrally controlled banking system, where a central bank makes monetary policy, and large banking institutions implement it under the regulatory guidance of the central bank. Such a distributed banking system can be designed as an online experiment for social networks, and gradually expanded into small physical communities such as college campuses, and entrepreneurial start-up communities. Such communities need to be protected from competition by big banks initially; but once they established, they would have to be opened up to competition to prove their superiority. Similar peer-to-peer concepts can be useful in experimenting with election systems and democratic institutions. But such experiments require new legal and social frameworks to encourage experimentation, to protect the experimental communities, and to protect the participants [11, 20].

Consider an experiment to eliminate all copyright protection laws. The common wisdom is that in such an environment, any digital product will be copied immediately and distributed widely with no remuneration for the developer. Consequently, there will be no incentive to develop complex digital products, destroying many industries from publishing to music and from movies to software. In fact, the outcome in a copyright-free society may be drastically different. It may lead to developers demanding much higher prices for their products, knowing that they will be shared, and selling very few copies. But those initial buyers are likely to be resellers and distributors, knowledgeable about the product and its market potential, and they have no incentive to give away the product for free. This process may repeat itself, with new resellers at each step trying to exploit the remaining market, and the price declining at each step, as the market is saturated. In this alternative scenario, all parties may be better off, by taking declining levels of risk as the market is developed, but also earning declining profits as the price falls, but all benefitting from the elimination of legal battles over copyright and the resulting exorbitant legal fees. Such an alternative can be feasible only if social networks and peer-to-peer markets allow anyone to distribute and resell digital products with minimal effort, and only if they can be protected from the existing copyright laws and vested interests that limit their ability to freely distribute and resell products. Such experiments require new legal and social frameworks to allow them to exist alongside the existing models.

Consider many religious cults that pop up frequently. Governments at all levels consider them a nuisance or even a threat to social stability, and harass them to no end. When in fact they could be viewed as useful experiments that provide valuable insight into alternative social arrangements such as polygamy, teen marriage, and homeschooling of children. Legal and social frameworks can be developed to allow and protect such experimentation, with some minimal regulation to reduce risk to participants while maximizing learning from their experiences [12, 19].

CHAPTER 25
CONCLUSIONS

The predominant mechanism of social learning throughout human history has been long-term competition among relatively isolated cultures. Each culture would adopt certain technologies, create social institutions and lifestyles to take advantage of those technologies, and then develop those institutions and lifestyles in relative isolation from other cultures. Periodically, the cultures would come into contact, compete economically, politically, and socially. Through such competition, they would evolve, flourish or diminish, resulting in human learning. Unfortunately, in a fast changing, high-tech, and global society, that mechanism of social learning is failing.

A technology-driven society is a society in constant flux and accelerating change. In that environment, traditions and cultural values become obsolete at an increasing rate, and lose their value as inter-generational learning tools. Social institutions become obsolete faster than they could be modified; and when they are modified, intense global competition favors short-term advantages, leaving little opportunity to develop complex social structures with long-term advantages. Markets become the dominant cure and the dominant religion to treat all social ills.

A proposal for social engineering has been sketched out to solve this problem. The solution involves comprehensive theories of interaction between technologies and social structures; and extensive experimentation with alternative technologies and alternative social institutions. Experiments are expected to rely on modern communication and coordination technologies; and they are expected to be protected from short-term competition from established technologies and traditional social institutions for long periods of time, to allow them to develop, and eventually to compete.

REFERENCES

Part 1:

1. Alcock J. Back from the Future: Parapsychology and the Bem Affair. *Skeptical Inquirer* 2 2011.
2. Balabanian N. Controlling technology: Should We Rely on the Marketplace? *IEEE Technology and Society.* Summer 2000.
3. Batie S., Mercuro N. *Alternative Institutional Structures: Evolution and Impact.* Routledge Publishing 2008.
4. Beavers A.F. *Exploring Ancient World Cultures.* University of Evansville Press Online Book 1997.
5. Carroll S. B., Grenier J., Weatherbee S. *From DNA to Diversity: Molecular Genetics and the Evolution of Animal Design.* Wiley 2004.
6. Chang H. J. *Bad Samaritans: The Guilty Secrets of Rich Nations.* Random House Books 2007.
7. Christensen C. M., Baumann H., Ruggles R., Sadtler T. M. Disruptive Innovation for Social Change. *Harvard Business Review*, December 2006.
8. Cross G., Szostak R. *Technology and American Society: A History.* Prentice Hall 2004.
9. Dawkins R. *The God Delusion.* Houghton Mifflin Harcourt 2006.
10. Dertourzos M. *What Will Be. How the New World of Information Will Change Our Lives.* Harper One Publishing 1998.
11. Diamond J. *Guns, Germs and Steel: The Fates of Human Societies.* W. W. Norton 1999.
12. *The Economist.* Virtual Economies. Jan 2005.
13. Ford M. The Lights in the Tunnel: Automation, Accelerating Technology and the Economy of the Future. Create Space Publishing 2009.
14. Furubotn E., Richter R. *Institutions and Economic Theory: The Contribution of the New Institutional Economics.* University of Michigan Press 2005.
15. Garrow C.E., Deer S. *Tribal Criminal Law and Procedure.* Rowman Altamira 2004.

16. Good P.I. Hardin J.W. *Common Errors in Statistics.* Wiley 2011.

17. Greco T. *The End of Money and the Future of Civilization.* Chelsea Green Publishing 2009.

18. Halperin, R. *Economies Across Cultures: Towards a Comparative Science of the Economy.* St. Martin's Press 1988.

19. Harris M. *Cannibals and Kings: The Origins of Cultures.* Vintage 1977.

20. Jacobson N. Escape from Alienation: The challenge to Nation-State. *Representation* 84, 2004.

21. Jeffcote R. Technology and Utopia. *Journal of Interdisciplinary and Cross-Cultural Studies* 3, 2003.

22. Knight J. Sened I. *Explaining Social Institutions.* University of Michigan Press 1998.

23. Loudin J. *The Hoax of Romance.* Prentice-Hall, 1981

24. Mowshowitz A. Virtual Organization: Towards a Theory of Societal Transformation Stimulated by Information Technology. *Communications of the ACM* 4, 11, 2-3, 2003.

25. Nelson R. On the Uneven Evolution of Human Know-how. *Journal of Research Policy* 32, 6, 909-922, 2003.

26. Orman L.V. The Potential of Virtual Institutions. *IEEE Technology and Society* 30, 1, 56-64, 2011.

27. Orman L.V. Technology as Risk. *IEEE Technology and Society* 2013.

28. Pearl J. *Causality: Models of Reasoning and Inference.* Cambridge University Press 2000.

29. Pinker S. *The Better Angels of Our Nature: Why Violence Has Declined.* Viking Press 2011.

30. Polanyi K. *The Great Transformation: The Political and Economic Origins of Our Time.* Beacon Press 2001.

31. Rosecrance R. *The Rise of the Virtual State: Wealth and Power in the Coming Century.* Basic Books 1999.

32. Rosen C. The New Meaning of Mobility. *The New Atlantis* 31, 40-46, 2011.

33. Sergienko G.S. The Ethics of the Adversary System. Bepress Legal Series 396, 2004.

34. Shulevitz J. Why Fathers Really Matter. *NY Times,* Sep 8 2012.

35. Staggenborg S. *Social Movements*, Oxford University Press 2008.
36. Steane A. *The Wonderful World of Relativity: A Precise Guide for the General Reader*. Oxford University Press 2012.
37. Sugiyama S. *Human Sacrifice, Militarism, and Rulership*. Cambridge University Press 2005.
38. Tainter J. *Collapse of Complex Societies*. Cambridge University Press 1988.
39. Taleb N. N. *The Black Swan: The Impact of the Highly Improbable*. Random House 2007.
40. Weil A. Health and Healing. Mariner Books 1998.
41. Zerzan J. *Against Civilization*. Feral House 2005.
42. Zerzan J. *Twilight of the Machines*. Feral House 2008.
43. Zuboff S. *The Support Economy: Why Corporations are Failing Individuals and the Next Episode of Capitalism*. Viking Books 2002.

Part 2

1. Andrews E. Christian Missions and Colonial Empires Reconsidered. *Journal of Church & State* 51, 2010.
2. Barmash I. *The Manipulated Society: How Advertising, Public Relations, and Mass Media Influence Public Opinion, Taste, and Purchases*. Beard Books 2009.
3. Beavers A.F. *Exploring Ancient World Cultures*. Evansville Press 1997.
4. Christensen C. M., Baumann H., Ruggles R., Sadtler T. M. Disruptive Innovation for Social Change. *Harvard Business Review*, December 2006.
5. Clark R. *Capital Punishment in Britain*. Ian Allan 2009.
6. Cross G., Szostak R. *Technology and American Society: A History*. Prentice Hall 2004.
7. Fishbein H.D. *Peer Prejudice and Discrimination: The Origins of Prejudice*. Erlbaum 2002.
8. Foucault M. *Discipline and Punish: The Birth of the Prison*. Random House 1975.
9. Friedman L. *Guarding Life's Dark Secrets: Legal and Social Controls over Reputation, Propriety, and Privacy*. Stanford University Press 2007.

10. Garrow C.E., Deer S. *Tribal Criminal Law and Procedure.* Rowman Altamira 2004.

11. Greenfeld L. Mind, Modernity, and Madness. The Impact of modernity on Human Experience. Harvard University Press 2013.

12. Harris M. *Cannibals and Kings: The Origins of Cultures.* Vintage 1977.

13. Hemp P. Death by Information Overload. *Harvard Business Review* Sep 2009.

14. Ingle S. *The Social and Political Thought of George Orwell: A Reassessment.* Routledge 2006.

15. Jeffcote R. Technology and Utopia. *Journal of Interdisciplinary and Cross-Cultural Studies* 3, 2003.

16. Knight J., Sened I. *Explaining Social Institutions.* University of Michigan Press 1998.

17. Krugler D. F. *The Voice of America and the Domestic Propaganda Battles.* University of Missouri Press 2000.

18. Lace S. The glass consumer: Life in a Surveillance Society. Policy Press 2005.

19. McNeill W. H. *The Pursuit of Power: Technology, Armed Force, and Society.* University of Chicago Press 1984.

20. Musto D.F. *The American Disease: Origins of Narcotic Control.* Oxford University Press 1999.

21. NY Times. More Demands on Cell Carriers in Surveillance. July 8 2012.

22. NY Times. The Woes at People's Express. June 25 1986.

23. Odlyzko A.M. The evolution of price discrimination in transportation and its implications for the Internet. *Review of Network Economics* 3, 3, pp. 323-346, 2004.

24. Olds J. *The Lonely American: Drifting Apart in the Twenty-first Century.* Beacon Press 2009.

25. Orman L.V. Technology as the Driver of Knowledge, Belief and Culture. *ICAST Journal* 2012.

26. Orman L.V. The Potential of Virtual Institutions. *IEEE Technology and Society* 30, 1, 56-64, 2011.

27. Pew Research Center. *The Decline of Marriage and Rise of New Families.* Pew Research Center 2010.

28. Reene J. *Stockholm Syndrome.* Betascript Publishing 2012.

29. Sifry M. L. *WikiLeaks and the Age of Transparency.* Counterpoint 2011.
30. Strandburg K. J., Raicu D. S. *Privacy and Technologies of Identity: A Cross-Disciplinary Conversation.* Springer 2005.
31. Taylor J. A. Zero Privacy. *IEEE Spectrum* **45**, 7, 20–20, 2008.
32. Wall Street Journal. The Internet Lets It All Hang Out. June 13 2011.
33. Younger J.G. *Sex in the Ancient World.* Routledge Pub. 2004.

Part 3

1. Adam G. Flying or Driving: Which is Safer? Science August 25 2010.
2. Ariely D. Predictably Irrational: The Hidden Forces That Shape Our Decisions. Harper 2010.
3. Belobaba P., Odoni A. Barnhart C. The Global Airline Industry. Wiley 2009.
4. Bernstein P.L. Against the Gods: The Remarkable Story of Risk. Wiley 1998.
5. Boyle D. *Funny Money: In Search of Alternative Cash.* Harper Collins 1999.
6. Cross G., Szostak R. *Technology and American Society: A History.* Prentice Hall 2004.
7. Donnelly J.S. *The Great Irish Potato Famine.* Sutton 2001.
8. The Economist. Virtual Economies. Jan 2005.
9. Ewald P.W. *Evolution of Infectious Disease.* Oxford Press 1996.
10. Ford M. The Lights in the Tunnel: Automation, Accelerating Technology and the Economy of the Future. Create Space Publishing 2009.
11. Galbraith J.K. *A Short History of Financial Euphoria.* Penguin Books 1994.
12. Greco T.H. *The End of Money and the Future of Civilization.* Chelsea Green Pub 2009.
13. Halsall F. Computer Networking and the Internet. Addison Wesley 2005.

14. Huber J., Robertson J. *Creating New Money: A Monetary Reform for the Information Age.* New Economics Foundation 2001.

15. Joffe C. Dispatches from the AbortionWars. The Costs of Fanaticism to Doctors, Patients and the Rest of Us. Beacon Press 2010.

16. Krugman P. *The Return of Depression Economics and the Crisis of 2008.* Norton 2009.

17. Kahneman D., Slovic P., Tversky A. Judgment under Uncertainty: Heuristics and Biases. Cambridge 1982.

18. Lietaer B. A. *The Future of Money: Beyond Greed and Scarcity.* Century Publishing 2000.

19. Marean C. W. When the Sea Saved Humanity. *Scientific American,* July 2010.

20. McNeill W. H. *The Pursuit of Power: Technology, Armed Force, and Society.* University of Chicago Press 1984.

21. O'Boyle T. F. *At Any Cost: Jack Welch, General Electric, and the Pursuit of Profit.* Vintage 1999.

22. Ofek H. The Tortured Logic of Drone War. The New Atlantis 27, 35-44, 2010.

23. Orman L.V. The Potential of Virtual Institutions. IEEE Technology and Society 30, 1, 56-64, 2011.

24. Orman L.V. Virtual Money in Electronic Markets and Communities. ICAST Journal of Communication, Social Informatics, and Technology 2010.

25. Pearl J. Causal inference in statistics: An overview. *Statistics Surveys* 3, 96-146, 2009.

26. Pontzer H. Debunking the Hunter-Gatherer Workout. *NY Times,* August 24 2012.

27. Rothbard M.N. *A History of Money and Banking in the United States.* Ludwig von Mises Institute 2002.

28. Schoemer K.G. Change is Your Competitive Advantage. Adams Media 2009.

29. Science Daily. Dangers of Cell Phone Use. March 2009.

30. Solomon E.H. Virtual Money. Oxford Press 1997.

31. Taleb N. N. The Black Swan: the Impact of the Highly Improbable. Random House 2007.

32. Velasquez-Manoff M. An Immune Disorder at the Root of Autism. *NY Times* Aug 25 2012.

33. Weatherford J. *The History of Money.* Three River Press 1998.

Part 4

1. Andrews E. Christian Missions and Colonial Empires Reconsidered. *Journal of Church & State* 51, 2010.
2. Barmash I. *The Manipulated Society: How Advertising, Public Relations, and Mass Media Influence Public Opinion, Taste, and Purchases.* Beard Books 2009.
3. Beavers A.F. *Exploring Ancient World Cultures.* Evansville Press 1997.
4. Boot M. *War Made New: Technology, Warfare, and the Course of History, 1500 to Today.* Penguin Books 2006.
5. Chaliand G. Bin A. *The History of Terrorism: From Antiquity to Al Qaeda.* University of California Press 2007.
6. Christensen C. M., Baumann H., Ruggles R., Sadtler T. M. Disruptive Innovation for Social Change. *Harvard Business Review*, December 2006.
7. Davis H. *Search Engine Optimization.* O'Reilly Media 2006.
8. Diamond J. *Guns, Germs and Steel: The Fates of Human Societies.* W. W. Norton 1999.
9. Farrell W. *Why Men Are the Way They Are.* Berkley Pub. 1988.
10. Ford M. The Lights in the Tunnel: Automation, Accelerating Technology and the Economy of the Future. Create Space Publishing 2009.
11. Furubotn E., Richter R. *Institutions and Economic Theory: The Contribution of the New Institutional Economics.* University of Michigan Press 2005
12. Harris M. *Cannibals and Kings: The Origins of Cultures.* Vintage 1977.
13. Herman E. S., Chomsky N. *Manufacturing Consent. The Political Economy of the Mass Media.* Pantheon 2002.
14. Jacobson N. Escape from Alienation: The challenge to Nation-State. *Representation* 84, 2004.
15. Jones A. *Genocide, War Crimes and the West: History and Complicity.* Zed Books 2004.

16. Knight J. Sened I. *Explaining Social Institutions.* University of Michigan Press 1998.

17. Levine J. *Harmful to Minors: The Perils of Protecting Children from Sex.* University of Minnesota Press 2002.

18. Moore L. Rep. Todd Akin: The Statement and the Reaction. *NY Times,* August 20 2012.

19. Olasky M. *Abortion Rites: A Social History of Abortion in America.* Crossway Pub. 1992.

20. Orman L. Bayesian Inference in Trust Networks. *ACM Transactions on MIS* 2013.

21. Pinker S. *The Better Angels of Our Nature: Why Violence Has Declined.* Viking Press 2011.

22. Polanyi K. *The Great Transformation: The Political and Economic Origins of Our Time.* Beacon Press 2001.

23. Rosecrance R. *The Rise of the Virtual State: Wealth and Power in the Coming Century.* Basic Books 1999.

24. Russo A. Internet2. *Slate Magazine* June 7 2005.

25. Sergienko G.S. The Ethics of the Adversary System. Bepress Legal Series 396, 2004

26. Tracy J. *The Civil Disobedience Handbook: A Brief History and Practical Advice for the Politically Disenchanted.* Manic Press 2001.

Part 5

1. Balabanian N. Controlling technology: Should We Rely on the Marketplace? *IEEE Technology and Society.* Summer 2000.

2. Batie S., Mercuro N. *Alternative Institutional Structures: Evolution and Impact.* Routledge Publishing 2008.

3. Boland R.J., Collopy F. *Managing as Designing.* Stanford Business Books 2004.

4. Chang H. J. *Bad Samaritans: The Guilty Secrets of Rich Nations.* Random House Books 2007.

5. Cross G., Szostak R. *Technology and American Society: A History.* Prentice Hall 2004.

6. Dertourzos M. *What Will Be. How the New World of Information Will Change Our Lives.* Harper One Publishing 1998.

191

7. Diamond J. *Guns, Germs and Steel: The Fates of Human Societies.* W. W. Norton 1999.
8. *The Economist.* Virtual Economies. Jan 2005.
9. Ford M. The Lights in the Tunnel: Automation, Accelerating Technology and the Economy of the Future. Create Space Publishing 2009.
10. Furubotn E., Richter R. *Institutions and Economic Theory: The Contribution of the New Institutional Economics.* University of Michigan Press 2005.
11. Greco T. *The End of Money and the Future of Civilization.* Chelsea Green Publishing 2009.
12. Halperin, R. *Economies Across Cultures: Towards a Comparative Science of the Economy.* New York: St. Martin's Press 1988.
13. Jacobson N. Escape from Alienation: The challenge to Nation-State. *Representation* 84, 2004.
14. Jeffcote R. Technology and Utopia. *Journal of Interdisciplinary and Cross-Cultural Studies* 3, 2003.
15. Knight J. Sened I. *Explaining Social Institutions.* University of Michigan Press 1998.
16. Mowshowitz A. Virtual Organization: Towards a Theory of Societal Transformation Stimulated by Information Technology. *Communications of the ACM* 4, 11, 2-3, 2003.
17. Nelson R. On the Uneven Evolution of Human Know-how. *Journal of Research Policy* 32, 6, 909-922, 2003.
18. Orman L.V. The Potential of Virtual Institutions. *IEEE Technology and Society* 30, 1, 56-64, 2011.
19. Orman L.V. Technology as Risk. *IEEE Technology and Society 2013.*
20. Polanyi K. *The Great Transformation: The Political and Economic Origins of Our Time.* Beacon Press 2001.
21. Ridley M. *The Rational Optimist: How Prosperity Evolves.* Harper Publishing 2010.
22. Rosecrance R. *The Rise of the Virtual State: Wealth and Power in the Coming Century.* Basic Books 1999.
23. Rosen C. The New Meaning of Mobility. *The New Atlantis* 31, 40-46, 2011.
24. Stivers R. *Technology as Magic: The Triumph of the Irrational.* Continuum Publishing 2001.

25. Tainter J. *Collapse of Complex Societies.* Cambridge University Press 1988.
26. Taleb N. N. *The Black Swan: the Impact of the Highly Improbable.* Random House 2007.
27. Zerzan J. *Against Civilization.* Feral House 2005.
28. Zerzan J. *Twilight of the Machines.* Feral House 2008.
29. Zuboff S. *The Support Economy: Why Corporations are Failing Individuals and the Next Episode of Capitalism.* Viking Books 2002.

www.ingramcontent.com/pod-product-compliance
Lightning Source LLC
Chambersburg PA
CBHW070008300526
45794CB00001B/231